Life Unexpected

Shirley Mae

RoseDog Books
PITTSBURGH, PENNSYLVANIA 15238

RoseDog Books
585 Alpha Drive, Suite 103
Pittsburgh, PA 15238
Visit our website at www.rosedogbookstore.com

ISBN: 979-8-88527-575-0
eISBN: 979-8-88527-625-2

INTRODUCTION

My life was always a challenge for me, and it stayed that way for reasons this story will unfold!

I was not supposed to be here, but my mom had what you would call an oopsie. She joked that I was born with the pill in my hand. Besides being born butt first, I had a deformed lung, and they were not sure if I would live or not. Thinking back now, I feel that was some sort of message that I was in for a rough road ahead!

I was my mother's third child. She had some difficulty having children, and so when I was born, they fixed it so she would not have anymore.

My father was not happy about that and throughout the years it did affect their relationship, which will be revealed later in the story.

Also, being born in the time when World War II was ending, our life was not embellished with riches You would not think of my family being poor, but a little lower than what is considered middle-class.

Anyway, as my story has many twists and turns throughout my life, this made me wonder how I survived and became the person I am.

Before we go into my life story let me fill you in on the two people who brought me into the world.

CHAPTER ONE

My Parents

ABOUT DAD

My dad came from a family that involved stepchildren and step-mothers from hell. Over the years of his childhood, he was mistreated mentally and physically and treated like a slave by his stepmother. She constantly blamed him for anything that went wrong and for reasons unknown his father never stepped in to protect him from the abuse.

Dad was taken away from his birthmother at the age of two because (as I was told) she had a mental illness and had to be committed to a facility that could help her and, according to the stories he heard from his father about her, she was not all there (to quote him), he also admitted that he was the one who placed her in an institution.

Unfortunately, she never got better but, according to my dad, he claims he saw her drive by his home once and holler out the window, "I am your mother," and she drove away. Later his father told him that he could not have seen her because she was still in the institution. Shortly after that, his mother's illness got worse and eventually, she died from causes unknown.

Back to the wicked stepmother. She married his father because she thought he had money being a builder and contractor and seemed to live way above a middle-class lifestyle.

Dad was only about three years at the time, and she soon had a daughter that unfortunately was a bit slow in her mind and had to have special care. So, Dad was forced as he got older to do all the chores and look after her while his stepmother ventured out to do (whatever) during the day.

When Dad turned seventeen, she decided to kick him out for reasons Dad never revealed or else he was not sure himself why she did it and why his father did not stop it from happening. Dad was so upset that he left walking, forgetting that he had a car! So, he hitchhiked and walked until he was hundreds of miles away from home.

After a few days, he ran across an old barn and feeling cold and tired decided to hunker down in the straw for warmth and try to sleep. The next morning, he was awakened by something poking at him, which turned out to be a rifle held by a very intimidatingly huge man.

He tried to explain the best he could what happened and why he was there to the man. Slowly the man's demeanor softened and because Dad was so young and scared plus very cold, he told him to come in the house for some food before sending him on his way. While eating the conversation turned to Dad taking an interest in what the man was doing in his workshop.

After talking for a while, the man was happy to see that Dad had potential for learning his trade and could help him in his business of building things and selling them. The man told him that for room and board, he could work with him if he was interested. Dad took him up on his offer because he really had no other options, and this was a wonderful opportunity to be able to eventually learn a trade and support himself and in no way did he want to go back to the turmoil at home.

He stayed with the farmer for more than two years and learned not only how to design things working with metal and steel but also woodwork. Also, he learned farming skills and how to grow plants.

The list goes on and on and later it helped me understand why Dad had so many ideas in his head and constantly worked on all kinds of different projects but never stuck with anything in particular, or he could have gotten rich over the years. He was so artistic and inventive.

All that time he made no contact with the family at home, and for some reason he realized, because it did not appear that anyone was looking for him, that he was on his own for sure. This saddened him because he loved his father and wished he loved him back, but the upside of it all was he was not being abused anymore and this man that took him in made him feel worthwhile and like he could go on with life with a hope for a future.

ABOUT MOM

Mom was the oldest of a huge family (10 children) in a ridiculously small house with a big yard. It reminded me of (the little old lady that lived in a shoe except my grandma new what to do!)

Mom's parents slept downstairs in a very tiny bedroom and the kids all slept in the attic. The stairs were like a ladder, very steep, dark, and narrow.

The bathroom was an outhouse, so going out to the toilet at night was another scaring matter. Once there was a beehive up in the corner and while in there you hurried hoping the bees would not come down and sting you! In the winter it was put on the coat and boots and trudge your way to the "Back Forty" (that is want we called it) and hurry back to get warm in bed.

To wash up was usually the kitchen sink or a metal tub, which they used for bathing once a week. Being first to have a bath was a luxury according to Mom.

Her mom did laundry in a big tub with a washboard for scrubbing for many years and then eventually got a rinse tub with a hand ringer that squeezed out the water and then she would hang them up outside year-round. Sometimes in the winter she would string a line on the enclosed back porch to dry some of the items. If the sun was out, she would hang sheets and bulky items outside.

So, life was not easy, but my grandmother was a tough cookie and my grandfather worked hard as a mechanic and delivered coal to homes.

Mom was called upon to help with her siblings a lot and help with chores daily because her mother had a lot to deal with tending to the babies according to mom had a new one almost every year.

Sometimes she would get punished for things that the other kids blamed her for, and this built up resentment over time! She loved her parents and her siblings, but it was hard for her to maintain that love with how she was treated daily.

There came a time when they farmed her out to clean people's houses to help pay the household bills.

Even though her father worked two jobs, the pay was never great and with a large family, it was hard to make ends meet and her mother had to stay home to tend to all the kids.

She did that for quite a while until there came a time when she was mistreated by the people she had to work for and, if truth be told, the men who lived in the houses she cleaned (let me just say) tried to do things to her, even with the wives looking on.

She talked to her mom and dad about it and because of their financial situation they told her to try to avoid being alone with the men and do her job, but if it got too bad, she should tell the wife and then get out of there! This happened back in the '40s often and was never revealed because women feared that the men would find a way to destroy their lives and ruin their reputations. That sort of thing happened a lot and no one ever pressed charges!

HOW THEY MET:

Now during my parents growing up period they knew each other because they went to the same school and my dad did not live far away from my mom. He always liked her, and because Dad had a nervous speech disability when he was young, my mom would help him with situations at school that caused him problems and stood up for him when other kids treated him badly.

Mom also made sure he had a lunch every day because his stepmom hardly ever packed him one. He was very scared and nervous all the time and hardly talked to anyone but the teachers and her.

They would sit together, and she would invite him over to her house occasionally. He would help her with some of the chores and play with her siblings, which her mother appreciated. A lot of the time, he would not head home until dark because he knew what was waiting for him when he got there!

When Dad had to leave because he was kicked out, they both lost track of each other, but Dad told me he never lost interest in her and his goal was to go back and get her when he had a good-paying job.

Mom was in her late teens and Dad was almost twenty when he came back to where Mom lived. Her parents let him stay at their house for a bit because of how he helped around the house in the past. But of course, there were stipulations of him helping her dad with his work for room and board.

That went on for a few months before he revealed his true intentions for coming back. That was that he wanted to marry her and take her away with him. The talking did not go as planned, so they both left during the night and drove to another city miles away so her parents could not stop them and found a justice of the peace that would marry them. They were both young, but back in the late '30s and early '40s it was allowed if you were over eighteen, Mom lied about her age. She was close to being seventeen still underage. I guess they did not need proof back then, so the justice of the peace married them on the spot.

After a brief honeymoon, they went back to her parents' house to face the music and to their surprise the parents welcomed them back, most likely for the help the two could provide with the kids and chores until they found a house of their own.

They stayed and agreed to the stipulation and while there, they bonded over card games and beer nights and the ladies did quilting and sewing and sometimes joined the guys in the card games.

Mom got pregnant and my grandma got pregnant close to the same time, which seemed highly unusual and rarely happened, but it did.

Mom and Dad knew that it was time to find a place of their own soon. Dad was what you would call a journeyman in the field he was trained in and quickly got hired by a place that manufactured cars. Mom got a job working in a store part time and so they began to build their lives together.

They found a small house and Mom quit her job to get the house ready for the baby they were about to have. It was not easy financially, and Mom took in some sewing jobs to help make ends meet until it was time for my brother to be born.

Mom continued to do sewing jobs at home while raising my brother. From what I heard, he was quite a handful, as boys can be, but strong and healthy. It was not long after, that Mom got pregnant again. She continued her sewing job until my sister was born and then things got too busy for her taking care of two children to take in work.

Then Uncle Sam came knocking at the door, and Dad was drafted by the Army to fight in World War II. It was hard on Mom to suddenly be left alone to tend to all the needs that a house required, plus taking care of two little ones, but because money was tight, she took in ironing and sewing jobs to do at home.

Of course, it was a challenge to do work at home with two youngsters demanding attention, but back during wartime women were strong and resilient and just did things because they had to be done.

Dad was in the Army, and he told stories later in life about his adventures in France and Germany. He was a private first class and an MP and there was one time he had to oversee German prisoners. They were all on a train together and he got acquainted with some and he had a gun for controlling them but said he never had to use it. He said one time they stopped at a cotton field and the prisoners got out and helped a farmer pick cotton. I don't know if that was a for-real story or made up, but it was interesting.

He had served about two years of duty when he came down with yellow jaundice and was sent home on a medical leave. When he improved, which took several weeks, he got the notice to go back to base. His next assignment was to head back to Germany and train to become a paratrooper. He said he jumped out of the plane several times. After he got the news, he of course, told Mom and because he was over the jaundice, they could have a normal relationship. He was going to be gone for possibly a year or more.

Eventually, while tending to my siblings, Mom realized Dad had left her a gift before leaving. She was not sure for a while because she was told after my sister was born that the chances of her getting pregnant again were very slim. She apparently had a rough time delivering my sister and it left her with a lot of scarring.

Anyway, after checking with her doctor she found out that the impossible had happened. He told her that with the war and tough times, she should consider the news as a gift and that gift was going to be me.

Dad had no knowledge of this and when Mom wrote him of the news. He was excited and because he only had a few months left to serve he told her he would be home in time to help and be there for when I was born.

He almost did not make it, but the war ended, and he was sent home just in time for my arrival.

CHAPTER TWO

The Beginning

After Dad got out of the service, we settled in the Mitten State. He did odd jobs and we lived in a tiny house until he was offered a house that had a store and a gas station involved. So, he and mom started a business together with three small children.

It was not an easy adventure; Mom was kept busy plus trying to keep my brother, who was five, sister, an almost four-year-old, and two-year-old me under control so she could wait on customers. The customers thought we were all cute, so we were kind of a plus for business.

Dad was busy filling people's gas tanks and wiping windshields for most of the day.

I remember running around the store getting candy as a bribe to behave while Mom desperately tried to work around us to tend to customers. Back then a babysitter was not always available.

Eventually, Dad got a good-paying job doing the installation of metal ductwork that furnaces use, and this of course was in the field he was a journeyman at, so they decided to sell the place and they found a home that was better suited for a family of five.

Things were going along rather nicely from the stories that were told, until I was a little over three years when my tonsils flared up and surgery was inevitable.

Mom placed me in the hospital, but fear set in, and I started screaming! The nurses—who were dressed like nuns, by the way—

wanted to give me a shot. I fought them off until they pinned me down and it hurt!

The hospital was afraid I would scare all the other kids, so they kicked me out after that. I was happy to go home, but the fear of hospitals stayed with me for a long time.

So, my parents ended up taking me to the family doctor to have them out. Here I am, a tiny three-year-old in a strange place with strange smells and a scary man in a white coat placing me on a cold table.

I remember getting groggy and then nothing, then I woke up crying and throwing up blood and then nothing again. I apparently came out of the anesthesia too soon; now a fear of doctors developed!

While home recuperating, of course at three years old, I wanted to play outside with my brother and sister, but my mom would not let me, so I commenced to scream, which of course hurt my throat.

Luckily, we were stocked up with popsicles and that helped soothe the burning feeling I felt in my throat. My mom put my head on her lap, and we watched *I Love Lucy* on our round-screen TV!

That helped my frustration of wanting to join my siblings outside temporarily, but of course I still cried because I wanted to have fun like they were. After a week or so, I was able to go out and play finally!

Soon my parents bought a bigger house just behind and to the side of a fire station. It was a nice roomy house, but when the sirens went off in the middle of the night, it definitely opened your eyes!

Time went by and one day while playing outside in the sandbox, a dog came up to me. First, he peed on me and then bit me in the nose. The tip of my nose was hanging off and I went screaming into the house. Mom took one look at me and rushed me to the hospital, and a few stiches later, it was back on leaving me with a scar that would remind me of the incident and now I developed a fear of stray dogs.

Dad was a volunteer firefighter and every year they would have a

Christmas party complete with a Santa Claus. It was something all of us kids looked forward to. I always got some sort of doll.

Once not really believing in Santa Claus, I hid under the dining room table and watched as our parents put out presents under the tree. Of course, I got caught and yelled at for being sneaky and they said I would be lucky if Santa brought me a gift for trying to catch him in the act.

I was definitely a believer when we opened our presents Christmas morning, and my sister had a bigger doll than me. Santa got even, was the thought in my mind. My folks took a picture, and it showed the pure disappointment on my face and my sister acting all happy about the big walking doll she got. I never doubted Santa again!

All was well until later, around the age of five, when I contracted rheumatic fever; I only know what I was told, because I was out of it for the duration of the disease. It left me with a damaged heart valve, which created a heart murmur.

My poor brother, however, had scarlet fever at the same time. My sister was fortunate not to have developed either disease. Mom had her hands full taking care of us for sure. Dad had little patience for anyone ill, so he busied himself elsewhere until all settled down. He just tried to stay out of the way because he just could not handle it. After we all got better, we started having more days of doing things and going places.

For example: my dad loved to fish, and we went in his metal fishing boat to the river often. When I was about seven, we went camping. Dad had purchased a nice tent with a floor in it and we all had air mattresses and sleeping bags, unfortunately it was not waterproof, so when it rained, we had to pile in the car to sleep. Luckily, he owned a station wagon! We fogged the windows up, but we were dry!

Well, of course, you cannot camp without some problems. Both my sister and I came down with the chicken pox and we had to stay out of the sun. So, the rest of the weekend trip we spent in camp, no fishing no nothing, you can imagine how that went over with two young energetic girls We played cards a lot. Sleep was hard because of the itching.

I saw a picture of me sitting on a picnic table with a sad look on my face. Finally, our weekend trip was over. Home never felt so welcoming before. I still was not quite over the chicken pox yet, so I still felt crappy, but home felt better than camping!

It was time for school to start up. All of us kids liked school. I felt mostly it was because we were able to be freer with ourselves away from the strictness of our parents while there.

My brother and sister were close in age, so they played with different friends and had activities that I was not included in. Therefore, I would spend time in my room playing what was called "little people," which is where you do the talking for your dolls and create family situations with them.

Of course, I was made fun of by them, and one time my sister, trying to make me feel better I suppose, tried to play it with me and she hated it. I did finally grow out of it as time went by.

I remember, around the age of eight, I had a friend that had a pond with pollywogs, and I wanted some. So, I took my mother's pennies in her penny jar and gave my friend money for them. Well, I got them home and of course you know what hit the fan.

I was driven by my angry mom to the girl's house and had to put them back in the pond and she let her keep the money and I had to do some chores at home to make up for my thievery. Also, my mom got so angry she spanked me, and I was sent to bed without supper. That was not a fun time at all!

Time went by and one afternoon while doing our chores, Dad was home and he and Mom got into it about something and the next thing we knew he had knocked her down accidentally (something about the broom) we never knew the whole story, but he laid her on the sofa because she apparently passed out. He then had us kids kneel by her and pray she would be all right. She woke up and wondered what was going on and Dad told her they were arguing while she was sweeping the floor and she suddenly passed out. You could tell by her face that she did not really believe it, but she decided to go back to her cleaning as if nothing happened. Us kids just looked at each other thinking, *what just happened?*

That was just an example of some of the weird stuff that went on in the household every day!

Besides working at a store where he installed furnaces, Dad decided to raise chickens in the garage at one time, now that was an adventure. He raised them from baby chicks. He had quite the setup in the garage with heated lights and straw and about two mother hens and six babies. The eggs were a plus; Mom loved that part, but the makeshift henhouse was very messy.

As time went on, Dad decided to butcher them all when he did not want to deal with the mess anymore. It became too much work and not enough enjoyment. He would chop off their head and it is true, they run around after. I was shocked and amazed at the same time.

After all that was cleaned up, Dad turned the garage into a shop for making things to sell. Now, mind you, he had a decent-paying job besides being a volunteer firefighter, but he always wanted more and for some reason always needed to be busy most of the time. But even with all his hobbies and interests, he still found time to be with all of us after dinner. Like watching TV and eating popcorn, that was his idea of bonding with us.

Mom always had chores for us to do, but she, too, would put all aside and spend time with all of us after the dinner dishes were washed and put away unless she was upset about something and then there was hell to pay!

For example: one time my sister and I were doing the dishes and singing like we always did when we did chores together. Suddenly, out of the blue my sister started arguing with me about something and it turned into a yelling match. Well, Mom was not going to stand for that and so as a punishment she took every glass out of the cupboard and made us wash them all over again and said that if this bickering continued, we would wash all the rest of the dishes. So, we glared at each other, did the glasses, and shut up.

Another time, my brother and I were cleaning house, and he was chasing me with the vacuum hose and pinned me down and because I was screaming, he covered my mouth and my nose, and I could not breathe. I managed to wiggle out from under him, and at that time, Mom got home from work and heard all the commotion and got furious.

She had just bought a hanger (called a dowl) for putting curtains up and she went after me with it and spanked me first and then it broke, and he got spanked with the short end. He told me that what she used on him was more painful like the pain I had was nothing compared to his! I did not know why he even had to make that an issue. During the whole thing my sister just stood there crying and Mom said to her, "Why are you crying? Did you do something wrong?"

And she said, "No. I am just scared I am next." To say the least, my brother and I did not horse around or do much of anything together after that incident for fear of what might happen.

Now, my sister and I were not close, but extremely competitive in elementary school and we loved to sing. The school always had a talent show and we entered with one of our friends to sing a cute song. Mom made our costumes, which were matching. They were short skirts and very cute. Now remember this is elementary school, so it was all innocent. We sang a song that involved lollypops and we were the hit of the show. We licked the lollypops at the end. We had a huge applause!

Later in life I wondered if that came across as naughty to the men. I felt creepy when I thought about it!

Another time, I was about nine or ten and played a bride, again Mom made my bride outfit. She seemed to enjoy sewing and being part of the things we did in school. Anyway, the boy that was portraying the groom was very shy and when it came time for the pretend cutting of the cake, I had to elbow him. He was so red-faced I could not help but smile. School was always a lifeline for me, and I loved being able to be myself there. I craved being noticed, and being involved in plays and singing made me a very happy girl.

We were also involved in church activities. Mom and Dad sang in the choir; my sister and I sang together on special occasions at the church. We also sang on the radio channel that the church was on every now and then. Thinking back I feel kind of bad because, for some reason, I don't remember what my brother was doing back then. I don't recall him being involved in church activities much. Anyway, it turned out that the church was a fun place for me, and I loved going most of the time.

Between the church and school activities I have wonderful memories of the time spent with Mom and my siblings

Dad was too busy most of the time to get involved. But when he was involved, we all seemed to enjoy each other. But around the age of twelve, Dad started acting strange and agitated. I could hear Dad and Mom arguing about something involving a move. He wanted to move down south and with his type of work, he could get a job easily anywhere.

One day, I was staying after school for an activity and Dad was to pick me up. Well, when he got there, I noticed the car had suitcases and a cooler in it. I asked what that was all about, and he said, "We are heading down South to look for a place for all of us to move to. I am tired of this wintry weather."

I asked where Mom was and why she was not going with us. He said, "She had to work, and we would only be gone a week; plus, this way, you can meet your grandfather and step-grandmother that live down there."

I was totally scared and confused. I did not understand why I could not go home first, but it was my dad and he indicated it was okay by Mom to do this adventure, so off we went. It was a two-day trip. We slept in the car one night and drove through the next then when we finally got there we settled in a motel.

The next morning, he took me to his father's house, and I met him and my step-grandma. She was a piece of work and did not appreciate the unexpected visit, so we left almost immediately back to the motel!

That is where my nightmare began. I did not mention that the motel only had one bed. The first night was not anything unusual but the second night dad started approaching me in ways I was not comfortable with. This made me extremely nervous and unsure of what was happening. While Dad went to his new job, he insisted that I wash his clothes and get his meals, which was quite the project for a twelve-year-old. At night he watched a little television with me and then he would go to bed, and being young I was too energetic to sleep, so I kept watching television and in my mind was putting off getting into bed until I knew he was sleeping. When I finally did get in the bed it woke dad up a bit and he tried to get close to me in ways I did not understand, but he never forced anything just showed a lot of affection that seemed weird, and I was a little scared. I woke him up enough to tell him that I was not "Mom": He said he was not trying to frighten or hurt me just show me how he felt toward me. Now I really was confused and moved way over to the edge of the bed.

After the first night of us sleeping together, I tried to keep my distance from him, and I tried to let him know if I was uncomfortable about how he was acting toward me and that none of his actions seemed right!

I kept hoping that we were going home soon.

After about a week of this, Dad decided to keep the job and move us down South. On the two-day drive home, again sleeping in the car one night, he asked me to keep quiet about the advances he made toward me! Then he said he did not know what came over him and he would not try anything like that again. Of course, I believed him!

After we got home, he let my mom know that he had a good-paying job waiting for him and a house already picked out, and so, against her wishes, he uprooted our lives from the cold climate to a warm one.

That part was good, but Mom was upset on how Dad took me away without any warning and that almost broke up their marriage, but he managed to explain it all in a way she accepted, and I said nothing about how he acted with me; for the sake of the family staying together, plus he begged me not to.

The sad part about moving away was having to leave our friends and the fun activities that we were involved in. So, now it was time to adjust and make new ones and, of course, being young we found a lot to do, and it was exciting to see all that a new state had to offer.

Mom was having trouble adjusting to the move. She brooded about it at first! I could hear them having heated discussions about how he handled everything without her but eventually she adapted to the idea and started making the place homey!

Our school was just down the road from us, and a ballpark was across the street and a huge field of cows and bulls too. Our neighborhood was in a large circle, so we had neighbors in the back and the sides of the house, but with quite a large yard between.

The circle was fun for bike riding and other activities that were close by.

One day, while at school, I sat on a scorpion, not knowing he was on my chair and luckily (even though it hurt like hell) it was not poisonous! The class thought it was entertaining and a classmate scooped it up and put it in a jar so everyone could look at it. I did get sick later but only for a couple of days.

I believe I was the adventurous type because every once in a while, I would do crazy things that were not very safe.

For example: on the way to school, on a dare, I ran through the Brahma Bull field, which was on the way to school. I had a ponytail with a red scarf in it that flapped around while I ran. I heard yelling, "Hurry! It is right behind you!" I barely made it to the fence with the bull snorting behind me. It was scary, but I was the talk of the day at school. I liked the attention, even though I got a talking to by the school principal and, of course, got yelled at by my parents when they found out what I did.

Another time, just for fun, my sister and I laid out in the yard on a blanket trying to be still just to see how many buzzards we could collect in the sky above us that thought we were food. Well, that ended fast when they started circling closer to us and a big one joined the group. We giggled about it later, but I must admit it scared the crap out of both of us.

After we were there for a while, Dad built a cage on the back of the house so I could have pigeons for pets. Although they were not really what you would call pets, because they would not let me touch them. They would fly off and circle back to the cage every night to feed and nest. They were fun to watch, and it gave me something to look forward to after school.

Eventually they started having babies and then something happened that grossed me out. Dad wanted to make what was called "squab pie" which meant cooking the babies with vegetables and putting them in a pie crust. Well, I refused to eat it and was sent to bed with no supper because of my rebellion. Dad did not seem to care that I thought of them as pets and that is why I thought the whole thing was gross and cruel!

There was a time when the birds got in the neighbor's car when they left the windows down and pooped all over the inside. They yelled at my dad, and he eventually took the cage down so the birds would not come back. I was a sad, but I tried to understand it and eventually got over it.

There was never a lack of things that needed to be done. We had to work in the yard a lot doing weeding mostly around the rose bushes that grew along the side of the carport. That was not a fun job because the red ants would get on your legs or arms, and they felt like fire when they sat on you. Luckily, we only had to do it a couple times a year. My mom never seemed upset that it was hurting us, but she did slather us with calamine lotion when we were done weeding. Trust me, we weeded fast and furious to get done and prayed to God for strength to get through it.

Because of that and the fact that if my mom had an angry moment over something us kids did, she would make us go cut a branch off the bush and use it as a switch. The thorns hurt when they hit bare skin and luckily that only happened one time because when she saw the blood, she came to her senses, realizing she was really hurting us and stopped.

As we grew into puberty, my two siblings started to hang out together a lot without me, their baby sister tagging along, so I started to feel like I was being left out and ignored again!

One time I was in the backyard after supper to check to see if one of the fruit trees had any fruit on it, when I was knocked down. At first, I was in shock and then I was aware of what happening and as I was fighting off the guy that was attacking me, he stabbed me in the side of my waist, and I managed to kick him and screamed as loud as I could, and he ran off when he heard my dad yell "What's wrong" as he was coming out the door. He was trying to rape me but thank God my parents got to me in time!

I was bleeding, but he had only grazed me with the knife, and it just needed a couple stitches to fix it. Other than that, it looked like, he failed (thank God) to have his way with me! So, other than a description of him (which was hard because it was dark), he left no evidence to go on! The police tried to find the guy to no avail., Now, I started being afraid of going out at night for anything by myself!

Another scary time was on one of our swimming trips to the ocean. I was swimming and bouncing with the waves when something floated toward me. I thought it was someone's swimming goggles, so I picked it up and this gooey stuff ran down my arms and it started to feel like fire. I ran by the lifeguard in shock to tell my mom and she thought I was just pitching a fit and made me sit on the blanket. I crossed my arms and cried then, thank God, my brother ran up and said she is not lying it stung my foot. So, they asked the lifeguard what it was, and he told them it was a Portuguese man of war jellyfish, and they need to get me to the doctor. Luckily the poison did not reach my heart, but it did cause some scarring on my arms.

Later on, while on a group hike in the Everglades, I was walking along the swamp trail and my foot slipped into the water's edge and unfortunately there were baby water moccasins in the water. One bit me but the guide was able to suck out the venom so other than a small scar I was okay. As you can tell my adventures as a kid could have been my demise but, apparently God had other plans.

Now, back to my siblings! Many times, they would not include me. My brother and sister became best buds. They would go biking together and not ask me to join them, a good share of the time! I would go riding but mostly on my own or with neighbor kids. Anyway, I felt like a lone warrior most of the time and not part of their crowd.

I started visiting the boy that lived behind us. I mentioned before the yards were huge between houses. Anyway, he also went to the same school that I went to. We started biking together and whenever he played ball at the field across the street, I had to go watch. He was my first real crush, but I had to keep it to myself because my dad would not tolerate it or even allow it (come to think of it).

When 8th grade was ready to graduate, the school had a dance party for us and I got all dressed up in a pretty blue dress with patent leather shoes and curled my long hair that I usually only wore in a ponytail, so this time it was down and beautiful, at least that is how I felt. I went to the dance, but I did not dance with anyone. I was shy and became what people called a wallflower.

While living down South, Dad always treated me different than the other kids! His hobbies always seemed to involve me and me alone it seemed. He was into painting, taking pictures, and sometimes home movies. He would have me hold still in various positions so he could take what he called (still-life photos). I was happy that I could do things to make him happy and put him in a better mood than when he came home from work.

He would sometimes make me act out things so he could video them. It was kind of fun, but it felt weird and some of the stuff he had me do did not seem right. But again, he was my dad, I trusted him, and I really had no clue at my age what his thoughts were in asking me to do some of the things he requested.

Of course, he always did these things when we were the only people at home and because he asked me to keep it to myself or we could not spend time together anymore, at the age of almost fourteen and being naïve, I kept it all to myself. I wondered, though, if Mom suspected these things were happening. She always acted snippy with me and if I did something wrong, she would grab my ponytail so I could not get away and proceed with the punishment, which usually was slapping or sometimes the belt.

For instance, there was a time I got a failing mark on my report card for not finishing a sewing project. She did not even wait for an explanation; she just started yelling and grabbed me by the hair and took a belt and started wailing at my legs. It really hurt and I was bleeding. She looked down and saw she was hitting me with the buckle end of the belt. That was the first time she ever looked remorseful for the punishment; Dad was devastated when he saw what she did to me. He was threatening to take me away if she ever, ever, did that sort of thing again. Thinking what my life might be like if that happened, *Oh God please no* was racing through my mind!

When I went to school the next day, one of the teachers noticed a couple gouges in my legs and asked what happened. I was too scared to say, but at the same time, I needed to confide in someone because I did not understand why my mom got so violently angry at times.

The school principal discussed it with the teacher and finally they came over to my house and discussed this with Mom and Dad. He said he was not home when it happened and if he were, it would not have taken place. He said he would make sure it did not ever happen again!

Mom started being more careful about how she would punish me after that. Things like grabbing my ponytail and yelling in my face still happened, but the hitting was less and less, as time went on. I still always felt like I had to walk on eggshells around her. This made me want to be around Dad more for protection, but because of his infatuation with me that was not a good thing either. Life was confusing and tough at times for sure!

Mom hardly ever punished my brother or sister because they were older and not around home as much. They stayed after school a lot with outside activities, where, because of Dad's insistence, I was supposed to come home right after school.

After a couple of years, Dad lost his job for doing something that ticked off his boss, so instead of looking for more work there, he made the decision that we were moving back north to our old stomping grounds. This time he did not kidnap me and went on his own to figure stuff out.

We stayed behind to sell the house and pack up while he went back to where we came from to look for work and a house for us.

I was kind of relieved that he was gone for a while but sad we had to leave a nice warm climate because of him and whatever he did to tick off his boss so badly that we had to leave. I never found out the story behind that.

I neglected to mention that we had a dog that we brought with us in the move there. He unfortunately got run over just before we were ready to move back. It saddened all of us because we had him from the time, he was a pup.

Dad thought the neighbors ran over him because he would sit at the curb to itch or whatever a lot and because he was black it was possible, they did not see him in the dark since it did happen at night. He confronted the neighbors, but they had no recollection of doing it. Dad finally let it go because we were leaving anyway and there was no proof of foul play.

My brother and sister were more upset than me about the move because they were both in high school and had lots of friends. I was just starting junior high, and other than some school activities and friends, I was okay with it.

Dad found a house right next to my grandparents. (Mom's parents) What are the odds of that happening? It was a fixer-upper but very cute with a large yard and the thought of being near my grand-parents and aunts and uncles sounded like a great adventure.

Dad did get a job before we moved into our new home. It was at a factory that made cars and he did all sheet metal jobs. On weekends he would work on the house and us kids would help if we could. We had to use an outhouse because of no bathroom yet. It took considerable time to put one in.

We were all so glad when dad finished the bathroom! Yay no more out house.

It was not until later that my sister discovered what looked like a peephole at the top of the bathroom door. My sister pointed it out to me. I was not sure if that was a deliberate thing or a mistake in the building of the room, but anyway thinking about what it might have been for (to watch you bath) made me a bit sick, and so I made sure Dad was not home or otherwise occupied doing something out of the house during bathing time just in case she was right! We never mentioned it and just remained aware. We did not want to stir up trouble.

Anyway, the house turned out to be a nice ranch style with a huge carport big enough for two cars and a big living room with a skylight and a fireplace. Very stylish and we all felt proud of Dad's accomplishment.

One thing, though; he did a strange thing in the hallway he added padded walls and jokingly said that was for when we were angry. We could hit our heads on it and it would not hurt, but really it was a form of insulation to help keep the bedrooms off the hallway warmer. Still, we all thought, in our minds it actually could be an anger outlet!

When we had to enroll in school, we found out a couple of our aunts were in the same school. Remember I mentioned that my grandma had a lot of kids, and some were born around the same time my mother was pregnant.

On weekends, Dad was home more, and he and Mom would go over to my grandparents to play cards. Us kids were old enough to stay home by ourselves so we would make popcorn and watch TV until bedtime. Or we would go over and join in on the card games or just do activities with our aunts and uncles.

One time one of my aunts wanted to go to a drive-in movie. We made a paper bag full of popcorn and a thermos of Kool-Aid. We did that about once a month, and it was a blast. Once I hid in the trunk until we got parked. There was no seating room in the car at least that was the reason I was told I had to do that. It was a bumpy ride but felt adventurous!

Unless Mom had a list of chores for me to do, I would go over to Grandma's after school a lot and she would teach me how to can food out of the garden and learn how to cook things that Mom did not cook. It was the highlight of my day and helped me not think about some of the things I wanted to avoid thinking about, if you know what I mean!

Of course, Grandma knew nothing about how my dad treated me while growing up, and I did not tell her, even though I wished I could, but I was too scared.

One thing I was glad about was that Dad worked a lot on the job, so he was not home until dinner time, so he did not approach me in ways that made me uncomfortable very often. Also, he put in a huge garden, so us kids spent a lot of time harvesting and weeding every day after school! We did not have a lot of free time for after school activities.

We all started adjusting to our new circumstances, but it was not easy, especially for my brother. He left a girlfriend behind when we moved. My sister left behind some close friends.

I could not make friends because of my father's demands that I come home immediately after school.

Mostly I obeyed out of fear of unknown consequences if I did not abide by his wishes. Even though he might not be home from work yet, I felt he would find out somehow and I would hear about it or worse.

Mom and I still had conflicts between us, because of all the things that happened down South, and it was hard for me, and I felt like I was walking on eggshells around her most of the time just to keep the peace and not get into any kind of trouble that could bring out any unexpected flare-ups of her anger.

Her temper did not flare up as severe now that all of us kids were older and could stand up for ourselves, but there were those time when she would catch us off guard and most of the time turn the other cheek time would happen rather than have her anger get worse. My sister and brother blamed me at times for things that went wrong, and I would always say I did not do it, but I must have always looked guilty because my parents always believed I did whatever I was accused of and got the brunt of the punishment. Mostly verbal since, over time I learned how to avoid being hit!

After the house was rebuilt to Dad's liking, he decided to get horses and commenced to build a barn and a corral for them. We were all excited and eagerly helped to build it in preparation for the big event. He bought four horses—three grown and one colt, which I fell in love with and immediately took over the job of caring for. I left the bigger ones to dad and my brother and sister.

I did not like riding horses so that was all left for the others to enjoy. I enjoyed brushing and talking to the colt that I named Smokey, because he was gray with a white stripe down his face. So pretty.

One time while petting him I did not realize he was chewing on my winter coat's buttons. They were made of wood. Well, I went into the house not aware of the problem. When my mom suddenly started yelling at me, "What happened to the buttons on your coat?" She grabbed me and shook me making it hard for me to answer. Finally, I was able to tell her what I thought happened. Because it was so cold outside, I could not feel what he was doing and truly I had no idea that a horse would do that. I told her I would sew new buttons on the coat so she would not have to buy me a new one. That made me realize that Mom still had scary temper issues and so the stepping on egg-shells around her began again.

This caused me to act out in unusual ways. I say unusual because I loved animals and for the first time, I was mean and abusive to one.

My grandma's cat kept coming over to the house and Mom did not like him to come in the house, and he always followed me around, so while she was at work one day, I threw soap at him to get him to leave and it went into one of his eyes. It got infected. And I lied to my grandma and told her a bird must have attacked it. I felt bad but scared of the consequences if I confessed to what really happened.

The cat did get better, and I played with him outside and told him that I was sorry. On the upside, he did start staying out of the house and that pleased my mom.

After a few months, our neighborhood was voted in from township property to city property and my folks had to sell the horses right away. That was sad for all of us, and it took some time to find good homes for them. Smokey was the last to go and he was sold to a farm not too far away, so I could still ride my bike over to visit him occa-sionally. The only good thing that came out of that was it put the focus on other things besides Mom's anger and Dad advances. I was glad for the distraction.

Dad then decided to get into growing exotic plants and built a greenhouse to grow them in. Also, because we had a half-acre garden to grow vegetables. Apparently, he had a green thumb all his plants flourished. This kept him occupied and seemed to change the way he acted most of the time. He started treating me more like his daughter and we started doing things together more often. I even let my guard down a bit.

We both liked gardening and eventually he had enough plants and vegetables that we could sell some at the Farmers Market. It was fun, and it surprised me how many people liked what we had to offer. Because my parents always kept me in fear I was on the shy side and dealing with strangers on helping them buy things was hard for me. But eventually I got over my nervousness and started being quite the salesperson. I learned how to count the money they owed and make change back and for me as a very young teen helped my self-esteem grow!

During that period in our lives, I also decided to raise some ducks. Surprisingly my parents went along with it. I got four fuzzy baby ducklings and taught them to follow me and learned different commands that told them to come to eat or just follow me around the yard. We had a huge tub filled with water for them to swim in. Well, as you know baby creatures grow to be big creatures and long story short, Dad threatened to butcher them because feeding them was getting expensive, but I managed to talk him out of that, and we took them to a park and released them.

The farming project went on for about a year and Dad decided he had enough of all that and lost interest as he did with other hobbies over the years and tore down the greenhouse he built and downsized the garden.

Also, during the summer months, I became close to a couple of my aunts that were close to my age. We would spend time out in the vast yard laying on a blanket and covering ourselves with oil and vinegar to not only ward off bugs but get a tan. We would have our boombox blasting and lay out for hours. My one aunt would get so dark that it looked like her freckles just blended together.

Those were fun times.

Later one summer, my dad decided to buy some lake property and build a cottage so we could all go fishing and boating. It was about a forty-minute drive from the house. I enjoyed going there with all the fun stuff to do on a lake and we went there almost every weekend.

Dad and I used to compete on who caught the largest fish and later we would all have a picnic of grilled fish and chips and veggies. That was indeed a wonderful time in my life except for the constant fear of trying not to encourage any weird stuff toward me from either parent. For a lot of reasons, I could not totally relax around either of them.

The "BE CAREFUL NOT TO DO OR SAY THE WRONG THING" thoughts were always centered in my mind and took away enjoying life to the fullest for me.

Shortly after we started doing the cottage weekend adventures and it was time for school to end for the year, my brother was ready to graduate from high school and he managed to get a part-time job, but not in the field our dad hoped for. He wanted my brother to go into the sheet metal business with him, but my brother did not want that. My brother worked at a pet store for a while but then the bickering started up with dad still pressuring him to come work with him and so having had enough of the fighting he enlisted in the service. He needed to get away from the turmoil of Mom and Dad and their constant bickering and trying to control us and their attempts to stay married.

They fought all the time and her anger issues, and Dad's mental struggles were overwhelming for him, and he had had enough, so off he went within a few short months of graduating and unfortunately this left us girls to deal with it!

My brother's best friend from high school liked my sister, and before he went into the service they double dated a few times and became serious about each other. It did not take too long before he and my sister got married right out of high school. She was a year behind him in school but as soon as that diploma was handed over, they got married. Now I was left to deal with the parental trauma's

Not long after she got married, she discovered she was pregnant. You can imagine the whispers where some people assumed that they had to get married. In my mind I thought it was on purpose so she could get away from the never-ending problems that went on in our home. It did not matter how it happened!

Now I really felt all alone to deal with all the drama and work out how to escape the situation for myself. My sister and her husband settled in a town several miles away and began to build their family.

Being a senior in high school now and tried to stay busy and I even had some after school activities because now that I was older, I gave myself some freedom away from home whether my parents liked it or not. I finally was getting a backbone or so I thought. Some time went by and Mom had to have back surgery caused by an injury from years ago in an accident. And had to be in the hospital for a couple weeks.

I suddenly had to be home after school and fix Dad meals and keep the house clean for when she could come home. DEJA VU

This seemed to bring out the past-Dad personality again!

During my senior year in high school, I became friends with a male biology teacher. He was kind but also quite flirtatious with me. I liked the attention and in my young mind I started to have serious feelings toward him. He was single and seemed attracted to me. I always wore a dress or skirt and sweater to school, and he seemed to like the fact that I dressed in a grown-up manner, and he would talk to me about his feelings toward me and even suggested that we see each other seriously after I graduated. Occasionally he would give me little notes of encouragement that this indeed was a possibility.

I did not know this until after Mom was hospitalized that she found the notes I thought I had hidden well in my closet, but she found the box of notes in my room when putting my clothes in the closet and was going to throw it out but first (of course) her curiosity got the best of her, and she opened it. She was shocked at first' but she did not approach me about them, instead she took the box to my dad. He kept the box hidden until mom was hospitalize a couple days after the discovery.

A day or so after mom had her surgery, he approached me with concern and anger and demanded to know who wrote the notes and why I felt the need to hide it if it was all innocent.   I confessed that I had been hanging out with a teacher that was single and we planned on a future after graduation.

Dad's jealousy kicked in and he went to the school the next day and confronted the teacher. I later found out that he threatened his job if he kept on seeing me.

I went to see the teacher, and he said he could not see me anymore and that his job was on the line, but he did say after I graduated to call him if it was at all possible and to memorize his phone number so as not to leave another paper trail to be discovered.

Dad waited outside the school where the busses usually line up and honked at me to get in the car. I got in with a surprised look on my face and questioned what was going on. He said we needed to have a talk about this teacher who had been sending me notes. He wondered why I was interested in an older man. I told him that I enjoyed his compliments and that he would encourage me to succeed in what my interests were and that I felt I loved him and would like to date him after I graduated.

Well, that started a chain of events.

Dad drove into some big field and said, "If you want an older man to f—k you" I can do that." He started trying to undo my garter belt (which we wore back in my teen days to hold up our stockings) when I realized what he was up to, I was in shock. Instinctively, I slapped him hard and swore at him to stop or I would have him arrested.

To my amazement, he bolted to attention. I assumed my striking him and swearing at him, brought him back to reality and he stopped grabbing at me and started crying. He then started the car up and tried to get out of the field, but the field was muddy, and we were stuck.

We got out and started walking toward the road. He said we are going to either get a tow or hitchhike home. Mom was still in the hospital, so my defenses were on high alert, and I felt a bit afraid of what was going to happen next.

We ended up getting a ride home and I was tempted to blurt out what happened, but because I was able to stop it from going too far, I kept quiet about why we were stuck in the field. The people seemed suspicious anyway and I could see Dad was worried and scared I might blurt out something. But he was my dad, and he did stop, so I kept quiet.

Unfortunately, the feeling of all this with him was finally over, was false because when we got home, he got out his rifle and looked at me. I do not want to use this, so you need to never tell your mom or anyone else what happened today. I really felt he would not really go through with it but on the err of caution I told him I would not say a word, but he needed to leave me alone.

Of course, I was scared, and I feared him in the moment. I also told him that I would get a job as soon as I graduated and save up to find a place of my own and move out. He said good and nothing else. In my heart I knew he was not in his right mind, and I hoped he heard all I said and I was hoping for mom to return home soon.

Finally, mom came home from the hospital, and I ended up taking care of her until she was able to live a normal life, so it became a routine of me getting up then getting her settled for the day and then I would go to school. I would come home and get dinner and take care of her until bedtime. Back then people relied on family and did not hire outside help, so since I was the last kid at home, I was it for everything.

Dad worked extra hours to pay off the lake property he bought, but I could not help but feel he was avoiding having to take care of Mom and I hoped part of it was his feeling of guilt for how he treated me all these years.

I felt depressed about what Dad tried to do and took every pill in the medicine cabinet trying to end it all and I could not tell Mom why I wanted to end it all. Well, it was stupid and did not solve anything! What it did do is left me with a reminder of what I had done by damaging my ears drums (loud ringing called tinnitus).

Mom got terribly angry that I did it, but deep down she had to know the reason for why I did (that always stayed in my thoughts). Anyway, she lied to the doctor and told him I had the flu. The doctor prescribed some pills and I stayed in bed for a couple of days and went back to school.

I felt like I was suffering from a broken heart. I had no one to share my feelings with so eventually I started writing poetry and turning them into songs during the last part of my senior year.

I eventually learned how to play the guitar, because of the crush I had on Elvis Presley. Ever since I saw him once in person at a country show that some of the family went to in my early teens, I could not get enough of his music. I managed to get a signed picture of him after the show. I had to stand in line a long time, but when I got up to him, the smile that he gave me made it worth the wait.

I sang and played guitar while in the last semester of my senior year and was in a talent show, and though I did not win, I did get asked to play and sing at various occasions in classrooms or to entertain at school functions. Eventually, I was asked to play for the college in town for what we called "Hootenannies," which I was saving the money up to hopefully go on to college after graduation.

My mother made some of my outfits I wore for my singing adventures (Western Style) and I felt good and confident about appearing in public with somewhat of a professional look. My hope was to become a singer for a living, but I could not talk my folks into agreeing to support me in my dream, so I tabled it and started going to business classes to finish out the senior year.

Over time, my dad and I played guitar and banjo together and sang all kinds of old country songs. We had a better relationship thanks to music. That is one of my more comfortable times with him.

After graduation, I immediately was hired into a CPA firm as an intern.

I was so excited and felt like (at last), I can start my independent life. But unfortunately, something disrupted my life again. At the graduation, my friends that I spent time together with in school all got together and shared hugs, cold drinks etc. While we celebrated, and not knowing my best friend was sick, I drank out of her soda. I did not know until later how that was a bad idea.

My folks threw a party for both me and my aunt who was the same age and graduated with me. All was well and the party was great, but I slowly started feeling tired and not myself.

I started training to work at the accounting firm and it was okay at first, but I kept feeling exhausted all the time and developed a fever and bad stomach cramps.

In the meantime, my grandfather (on my dad's side) died. He lived in Florida. I stayed home, because of the new job! I did not feel it was right to leave on a long trip and besides, I really did not know him very well at all. I still was not feeling well either!

Both my parents seemed to be fine about my staying at the house alone! I did not let them know how sick I was because I wanted to be free of their drama for a while also being on my own in the house seemed like heaven to me.

Shortly after they left for the funeral, I really started feeling a lot worse and I stayed home from work because of a high fever and terrible abdominal pain.

My parents returned home from their trip and found me on the floor unconscious. I was rushed to the hospital.

It took a week for them to find out the problem.

They finally diagnosed me with an advanced case of mononucleosis. Because it took so long for them to figure out what was wrong with me the disease had damaged my liver and I was bedridden for eight long weeks. I had to go for blood tests every week and take giant, what I called "Horse Pills." I felt like I was at death's door and at times wished for it. I prayed every day for God to either give me relief or take me.

That was an ordeal that finally made my mother more compassionate toward me or so I thought! I tried to be on a friendship basis with her, but because of our history, I was always on my guard emotionally! I still could not relax around either parent.

Because she was sort of acting better around me during my stay-at-home illness, I decided to confide in her about all the issues I have had with Dad over the years. It was time she was aware since I did not want to take all this pain to my grave if I did not get better. Big mistake!

After I filled her in, I found what she said shocking! She said, "I knew it was going on, but I thought you went along with whatever he did because you liked it and you wanted the attention he gave you." I remember my mouth dropped and I just stood there in shock wondering how she could even think that a young innocent girl would go along with the stuff he pulled or even understand what it was all about. The thought of her thinking that about me made me sick inside! I hate to say it, but I developed a sort of hate toward her after that and it has left a wedge in my heart from that day on. I felt sicker after I realized she knew and did nothing to stop it.

Now she knows and seemed to have known all along, I felt terribly awkward around her and Dad whether they were alone or together. I had no idea what either was thinking when they were around me and I just wished I could just disappear at times.

The fact that she was taking care of me under what seemed like false feelings, I was at a loss and totally at her mercy. Also, what if she told Dad what I said to her just to get more leverage over me. It made me feel more uneasy than ever. I just kept quiet and hoped that God would give me the strength to endure whatever came next!

Luckily, my new boss agreed to hold my job position until I could come back, because he was a family-oriented person and knew I really wanted the opportunity he was kind enough to offer me right out of high school.

During the (eight weeks) the illness made me mostly bedridden, but I managed to take care of myself while my parents went to work. During the times that they were gone, I would get up and go outside and sit for a bit and write my poetry. I felt relaxed when I could write about what I felt and how I interpreted life in general and sometimes I would put it to song. I wrote this after the teacher infatuation. Example:

> *My heart has closed its doors.*
> *Its shutters are all pulled*
> *My life's an empty shell*
> *The feeling I know so well.*
> *The love I had has died*
> *Because of foolish pride*
> *My heart is filled with pain*
> *I'll never love again!*

When my parents got home, I made sure I was back in bed, and I tried to act like I was getting better and did not demand much looking after anymore. I constantly prayed that I would soon function normally again and get back to my new job. I was so happy they were holding my job for me; not too many companies would do that.

Mom took time off one day a week to take me for bloodwork and my checkup. Again awkward! Oddly she never brought up anything I told her again. I was relieved but still uneasy and cautious. *God get me out of here* was often my prayer.

Things were never the same between my mother and I after all was out in the open!

Finally, I got my strength back, I was able to go back to work, part time at first and then worked full time after a couple of weeks of my return.

Looking back (before I got ill) I was alone while my parents were gone and spent time with my grandparents, remember they lived next store, because they promised to keep an eye on me and make sure I did what I was supposed to do.

They saw me sit outside occasionally and I asked them not to tell and that really, I was still resting. Then on one occasion I told Grandma I needed to tell her something in confidence and she had to promise not to tell a soul. She said she would keep it between us, so we talked a lot, and finally, I confessed to her what I went through for years at home. She swore to secrecy and advised me to get out as soon as I could afford an apartment and told me her lips were sealed forever unless I wanted her to say something, but she would always be there for me if I needed a place to feel safe.

After that whenever I was not working, and no one was home, I would spend time at Grandma's house, and she would continue to teach me how to cook different meals and sometimes she would let me help her with household duties. She would tell me stories about how she took care of so many children and still did all the work around the house. I felt she was unstoppable!

I found helping her out on my off time from work very therapeutic and I grew more mature and less afraid of life and its possibilities thanks to her love and guidance.

If it were not for my grandmother, who listened to me, and believed in what I told her without judging me, I do not know where my life would have turned. She built my confidence up and always made me feel better about myself and my situation. Without her, my story would be different or not at all.

CHAPTER THREE

First Life Change

As I mentioned, after graduating from high school, I got a job at an accounting firm and started training to be a bookkeeper and accountant. It was an internship that I hoped would be a smart career move.

I worked in a three-story house, and they had me on the top floor. I was alone a lot but had to go down often with questions on the work they had me doing. Tedious but sometimes interesting.

While working, I met a young man who (as I learned later) was the boss's son. He was very handsome with dark hair and eyes not too tall but muscular in statue. To say the least he did catch my eye.

He did not work at the office but was helping to clear out the storage area of a bunch of files and boxes for his dad. We notice each other when I went to the storage area for a missing file that I needed for a client I was working on. He helped me find it and I thanked him and left.

At the time I had heard he was dating someone else in the office, so I stayed clear of him. Just did small talk when he was around.

After a couple months working there, I had to stay on a Saturday to answer phones and set up appointments for the CPAs when he stopped at the office to pick up mail and commenced to strike up a conversation with me. I greeted him politely and then I just, kept to myself. He said "I can see you are busy so I will talk with you another time"

A few weeks later, he stopped by again when I was doing the phone job and after a couple minutes of chatting, he asked if I was seeing anyone and wondered if I would go out with him sometime. Because I had to drive to the lake cottage after work, I told him that it was quite a distance and my parents always expected me home within a certain time frame. So that was my excuse for leaving work and going straight home. He seemed to understand but looked like he did not at the same time.

Time went by and on another day, he asked again if I would go out sometime and I said I did not think that would be a good idea. This time my excuse was because he was the boss's son.

He persisted a few more times, and finally I did go to lunch with him I felt awkward and tried to keep the conversation light, but after some time, I realized that we seemed to have a lot in common. (Plus, the chemistry was very evident between us)

We went out to lunch a few more times and then he wanted to do things that meant staying in town overnight. I discussed it with my parents, and it seemed that my mom was for it, but my dad grumbled a bit, and so I arranged for them to meet, and they both seemed to like him. They decided it would be okay once in a while.

So, we started dating after work, mostly dinner and a movie, then back to his folks' house After our dates I would drive to the cottage in the dark, which I did not like. Also, sometimes I would stay at the house next to Grandma's because it was not sold yet and it still had some furniture in it.

All was good in the beginning. He had me over to his folks' house for dinner a few times and we would lay on a rug in front of the fire-place and make out. Sometimes we would go up to his bedroom and lay beside each other and snuggle. He kept trying to go all the way with me and I kept putting him off, so he asked me to marry him in hopes that an engagement would make me more comfortable about having sex

We went out with some friends one night and then went back to his parents' house. After our friends left, he got down on one knee and holding a very shiny large ring ask me to marry him. I felt it would not only be a way out of my dilemma at home, but that we were meant to be.

I guess he was right because I finally did give in one evening to have sex and wouldn't you know it, his dad walked in the room and saw what was going on and walked back out. Awkward indeed, but we continued. It hurt because I was a virgin and luckily, I did not get pregnant. I went to a doctor right away and got on birth control pills.

We went out on several fun dates, but there were a couple times that were not so much fun.

Once while visiting my parents, we started roughhousing a bit and he rubbed his knuckles on my scalp (called a noogie) It hurt like hell, and I told him. He laughed and said I deserved it for whatever reason, I did not know. This should have been a warning sign of his personality, but, as they say, love is blind.

After he proposed. For some reason I was hesitant to set a date, but my dad seemed to push the issue and pretty much told me he wanted me to get out of the house. So, the wedding plans began. It was a mid-summer wedding and sure to be hot, the church was our venue and luckily well air-conditioned.

Picking out the dress was quite the challenge with all the people involved. I finally had enough of everyone's opinions and went on a day by myself and found a dress I loved and within my price range.

My sister lived in another part of the state, so I asked one of our friends to be my maid of honor and we also had four bridesmaids and he had the husband of our friend as his best man and four grooms-men.

Planning weddings, at least mine, turned out to be very stressful and not fun in the least. Like when I was trying to pick out a dress, there were a lot of outside opinions, so a lot of the time I just said OKAY to the arrangements, just to shut them up!

Even after all the stress and arguments the wedding turned out to be beautiful!

My dress was my dream wedding gown, it was A-line style and made of satin, with a beaded floor length skirt, and long lacey sleeves. A mental note (still have it in a box) the others wore short canary yellow dresses. The groom wore a white tux and the groomsmen wore black with white shirts. Of course, the reception was filled with dancing, cake and lots of gifts. Other than my mother saying I was not acting like she thought I should (too silly and giddy I guess) I felt like the wedding was all a dream, after all the things that never seemed to go well in my life.

Our honeymoon was very romantic, we went to an island up north that had horse rides and various things to do and we had fun most of the time, but then he did show a little bit of anger at me when I did not want to go along with him on something. But I have to admit mostly, he treated me like I was the love of his life. I felt hopeful that the future would be what I hoped for.

His parents owned a house in town and a cottage on a lake and since we did no house hunting before we got married, I did not know that he already made plans with his parents for us to stay at their cottage for a few weeks, until his folks wanted to move in there for the summer. They agreed to let us live in their house in the city until we found a house of our own.

I did not like the fact I was not consulted on the decision, but I kept quiet as I always did if not sure of the outcome.

All was well in the beginning but eventually I notice a slight change in how he treated me, especially when I wanted to state my own opinion on what we did and how we planned our lives. He acted very critical about anything I said and started being very demanding about how the house was kept up and how I cooked meals and mostly (WELL) anything I did.

A week or so after the move, he got worse. It turned into more of what you would call bullying. He would start in on my cooking, how I did laundry—his parents had a ringer type washer, and I accidentally got my hand with the wedding ring on it suck in it, and it bent my ring into my finger. Luckily, it only cut it a bit but messed up the ring, so it had to be repaired. Instead of being sympathetic about the accident I got yelled at because of what it did to the ring. He slammed his hand on the kitchen counter and gave me a chilling look and that is when I started feeling a bit scared of him!

After we were married a couple months, I caught him looking through my purse, supposedly for some money (like he did not have any) when he found a packet of pills. He looked at the label and found that they were birth control pills. He became enraged and flushed them down the toilet! He wanted kids immediately and I did not. Well, that is when the hitting and verbal abuse started up.

AN EXAMPLE OF SITUATIONS THAT TRIGGERED HIM:
One Sunday morning before going to church, I was suffering from a terrible migraine headache. His face got kind of twisted with his tongue jutted out to the side, and I could see the anger welling up. He commenced to jerk on my arm and slap me on the back and said, "Get out of bed; we are going to church, and if you say anything about me slapping you to anyone there, I will deny it since you don't look like you have a mark on you. And if you do, trust me; there will consequences when we get back home!"

Well, it was not just slapping it was the verbal degrading words that came out of his mouth! I made the mistake of telling him how I was treated at home and some of how my dad acted with me and he started accusing me of not being a virgin when we got married even though I told him it did not go that far and he started treating my parents differently.

Of course, I instantly regretted telling him anything and started keeping most of my thoughts to myself as I did in the past, from then on.

That confrontation brought back to the surface the memories of my childhood treatment to my mind and bit of fear set in.

Unfortunately, my husband wanted to be the controller of my life and if I did not do as he said he would either slap or hit me and, of course, always in areas that were covered by clothing (Thinking back to my life as a child) Once again, I had a man in my life that wanted me to do what he wanted and for me to accept it and I had to go along with it and not be my true self. TRAPPED AGAIN!

One time, when his parents came for dinner, I observed how his father treated his mother. She was helping me in the kitchen, and he did not like something she did, so he yelled some obscenity at her and kicked her in the ass when she left the room to help set the table. NOW I KNOW where this behavior came from, of course being in love, I thought I could change him, sound familiar?

One summer we were invited to a party at his parent's lake cottage, and I told him I was not feeling well. He again yelled at me and said, "Stop looking for excuses to get out of going and get your ass in the car." I pulled myself together, knowing what would happen if I didn't do what he said!

While at the gathering, I started throwing up and almost fainted. His mother stepped in and asked how long I had been feeling like that and I told her a couple of weeks, but that I did not tell her son. She explained that she thought I was pregnant and to see a doctor soon. Back then they did not have pee-sticks, it was blood test only.

She mentioned the possibility to my son and his whole manner changed like he had been handed a wad of money. After the doctor confirmed that I was pregnant, he became the man I wanted at last. Caring, helpful, and not hitting anymore. I kept my guard up!

During this time, we found a house together and finally had our lives to ourselves and not under the wing of his parents.

He concentrated on fixing the place up and sold his sports car, after I was almost thrown out of it on big dip in the road (no seat belts back then) and I was about six months pregnant, to pay for building a garage and a fireplace. He was quite the handyman! The memories of those days were mostly wonderful, and I felt life was good.

When we would disagree, he would state that his way was what was going to happen and I was smart enough to just agree and give him praise, if it felt like I should, and things went along smoothly!

Soon after the move, our son was born. He came out feet first and his little feet were bent at the ankles, which meant he would need some physical therapy to straighten them out before he could walk. Because he had some physical issues and the look in my husband's eyes, I could see the disappointment that I did not produce a totally healthy son and, of course, it was all my fault and from my side of the family.

Shortly after my son was born , I found out I needed my wisdom teeth removed. They knocked me out and took both sides at once. I was totally out of it, so my mom came over to take care of the baby and me if I needed it. I remember her being short-tempered with me even as an adult. She snapped at me if I asked for something, but she was sweet to the baby.

Again, I could feel her resentment toward me, just like when I was a child. It saddened my heart that she had not changed over all the years!

My husband kept his temper in check most of the time while I was caring for our son, I had difficulties nursing because of inverted nipples so after about six weeks of torture trying to get my body to cooperate, I had to resort to bottle feeding with formula. I was an emotional wreck and felt like a failure as a mother

My husband would still yell bad things at me, but he did not hit me. So, we grew a little closer and he loved playing with our son. About a year or so later, because we were getting along for the most part, I got pregnant for our second child.   He was delighted and treated me with kindness during the early stages of the pregnancy, because he came from a big family, and he want one.

Around the age of two, I noticed that my son had crossed eyes. When he was born they looked that way but we thought that they would straighten out over time, but they did not, so he had to have surgery to correct the problem.

I was delighted that the problem came from my husband's side of the family, but I kept that thought to myself! We both found out that some of the other boys in his family were born with the problem, so now he knew he was not from people who were perfect. I relished the thought! But as always, I just kept it to myself. I was just glad the problem could be fixed so my son could see properly.

My being pregnant, made his moods better for the first part of the pregnancy. But that did not last long!

When I was around six months along, he started being critical again and jerking me around and would slap me a bit but not hard enough to hurt the baby (thank God), if I argued about anything he did not agree with.

Thinking back, I remember that he never was violent with our son and mostly left me to care for him and discipline if needed. He worked a lot of hours and was on call at times, so when he was home, he expected me to take care of the house chores and our son no matter how I felt. So, I made sure I got things done and then laid down with my son if I needed to rest, if he would cooperate if you know how babies are that does not always happen.

One time, while still pregnant, my husband's attitude and temper got so scary, I escaped the house and started walking. The weather was warm so I felt I could do it. If it was winter, it would not happen.

I decided to go to his parents' house and let them know what was going on. It was a couple of miles, but I did not want to risk losing the baby because of his temper. Walking was probably not smart, but I rested after every couple of blocks and I made it to their house very tired but okay.

When I got there, his mother was home. I told her what was happening and to my surprise she was not sympathetic at all! She said that his dad was like that (which I knew already) so over time she just kept her opinions to herself and just went along with whatever he wanted. Well, this was not me! NOT AFTER HAVING TO BURY MY FEELINGS WHILE GROWING UP!! I know I had no choice but to head back home but I feared what kind of greeting awaited me!

After the realization that I was not even getting a ride back home, (My mother-in- law did not drive) and I was not about to call my husband, no way, I commenced walking back, I was hoping his anger had subsided.

In the meantime, he must have gotten a little concerned because of how long I was gone and because I was pregnant, he called my dad and had him look for me. Apparently, he did not want to himself for whatever reason, but I was too scared to go home anyway.

My dad came looking for me on his motorcycle and when he found me, I told him a little about why I left, and that I did not feel comfortable about going home yet.

He wanted me to get on the bike and I told him that I did not think I could with my six months pregnant belly He chuckled and scooted forward on the seat and made room for me. I reminded him that I did not want to go home yet. so, he took me for ice cream. (To me that was shockingly sweet and not at all the dad I remembered)

So, we went for ice cream, and we talked. I told him how I was being treated and to my amazement he was sympathetic and somewhat angry and confused as to why I did not let him know sooner. I told him I was not sure he would care. And he softened and said he was sorry, but because of our past, he understood why I felt that way. I felt like he finally was a dad to me!!

Eventually, he talked me into going home and he said he would have a talk with my husband about cooling his jets. He told him to stop taking his anger out on his daughter or he would be back to do more than just talk.

I was worried that after Dad left, I would get a beating for exposing the lifestyle I had with him, but he just said he wished I could just be the type of wife he wanted, (which was a yes-sir person) but because of the baby and our son he would try to back off.

No apology for his actions at all, he just said I brought out the violence in him because of how I acted. So, in other words don't have an opinion and all would be fine.

When our daughter was born, it was a rough delivery and they had to drug me up because I would not dilate for her to come out, so when she was born, I was goofy and she was a happy baby probably the stuff they gave me affected her too!

My husband was delighted that she was physically healthy and that now we had a boy and a girl which was what he was hoping for anyway. It always seemed to be what he wanted. Never mind what I was hoping for, which was the story of my life.

When I got home from the hospital. I now had a two-year-old and an infant to care for. Tried nursing again, but could not, so the failure feeling was there again, but I made myself get over it and bond with her over the bottle feeding. My daughter kept me up all hours of the night, unfortunately she had colic.

So, with my migraines, (which I had frequently) it was tough to function without help. Meaning, I could not call a baby sitter whenever I was not up to par so I just dealt with it the best I could!

I stared at my beautiful daughter and tried to be patient about her being colicky, but it was not easy. At times she would cry uncontrollably and if I had a migraine, I would have to close the door and let her cry, because I did not feel well enough to take care of her. I would grab my son and lay down with a pain pill for a few minutes and when the pain was less, I would get up and tend to her needs. I felt like I was being a bad mom for doing that, but I was so sick I felt I had no choice! This happened a lot while the children were little.

Eventually my husband allowed me to go back on birth control, but I found out that I could not take them for long because it increased my migraines, and I was even sicker with them when they happened. So, I had to stop taking them, and we tried other methods, like the rhythm method and some foam stuff that apparently did not work as well because shortly after stopping the pill, I got pregnant again. My husband was delighted because as I said before he wanted a big family.

Almost five months into the pregnancy, I lost the baby. It was a girl, and she would not have survived anyway because it looked like she would have been deformed and would not have made it to full term or survived if she did.

I named her Christine and did not have her buried in a plot and to this day, I never told my husband that I named her. He probably would have thought I was not in my right mind, so I kept it to myself it seemed to comfort me to know she would have had a name had she lived.

He did not go with me to the doctor's that day (job always came first) and I ended up in the hospital for a day. He came up to the hospital after it was all said and done, and I told the doctor that I would tell him what happened. I let him know that it was a miscarriage and that the baby was not developing properly and, for some reason the baby aborted itself. I was crying so much that he forgot to ask the sex of the baby until later! He did feel bad about it, but I don't think he understood totally why it happened. He did not say but I could see that he probably thought it was all my fault that the baby was deformed. So again, I felt like a failure.   After the shock of it all, I felt maybe God was saving us from more anguish by taking her before she was born instead of having us deal with whatever her birth problems would have been.

After a couple months of healing, he wanted to try one more time. I did get pregnant one more time, but I had a tubule pregnancy and miscarried almost immediately.

. This is where the egg would not attach to the wall of the womb. It attached to the lining of the tubes instead, so when it got fertilized it would not be able to develop and more miscarriages would happen.

This happened several times and the doctor recommended that I not try anymore because it would continue to happen. My husband was devastated and angry at the same time because he wanted a big family. I felt sad because one more would have been okay, but I felt our two were a blessing.

The doctor suggested I get my tubes tied or he said my husband could get a vasectomy. Well, that was not going to happen because in his mind if something happened that I was not around or as he put it, we split up, he would like more children. Well, that felt like a slap in the face and told me where I stood in his eyes. Like he had a plan already that our marriage was not going to last!

His verbal abuse was elevated after that, and the hitting started again. The bad headaches started again and more severe! I prayed a lot, not only for less headaches but for the strength to find a way to get out of the mess I felt I was in.

The kids started realizing how debilitating my headaches were and when I would have one, I would lay on the sofa, and they would take turns bringing me cold cloths for my head and play quietly so I could sleep. My daughter especially liked playing nurse.

On days I felt good, I worked out in the gardens while they napped, and the dog and I would be outside. Their bedroom windows were open so when they woke up from their naps, they would let me know and they could join me outside and either play with the dog or toys. Sometimes they even wanted to help me work in our vegetable garden.

Once while weeding, I was next to a rock I had positioned nearby to put my drink on, a squirrel sat on it and at first, I was not sure what to do, but all he did was look at my drink and took off when the dog showed up. The kids thought it was quite neat and hoped it happened again, which it did often. It was cute!

On sunny days we would go for long walks and talk to neighbors on the way. Those were good times! I loved the good days of fun and laughter.

I started having fewer headaches, but when the black cloud came over (which I called my husband's anger moods) the fear would take over and the good times ended with a blow (literally). His anger would trigger one of my bad headaches and I found solace by going to bed and, he would back off and take care of the kids so I could sleep. I think he enjoyed my being out of the picture, so he had the kids all to himself.

For some reason he started being sympathetic when I had a migraine. That was the only thing that made me (strange to say) kind of glad when one struck.

Now that the kids were getting older, more arguments seemed to come about and the verbal abuse started up again, but he did not hit me as often" thank God!"

The kids were in school now and I had some free time to myself, which I loved, but still had to make lunch for my husband every day and look like I had done something around the house and not just watched television. The house always had to look clean and no dirty dishes in the sink.

Once he got angry over something I did wrong in his eyes, and he tried to throw me out the front door. The neighbors saw what was happening but did nothing to stop it. Our daughter tried to stop him from shoving me out the door and, afraid he would hurt her, I reached back and pushed her away.

She fell back and started crying, and he yelled, "See what you did, bitch?" and kept pushing me until I begged him to stop by saying I would do what he wants. Because of the shock of it over time I have blocked out what it was even about. Again, no neighbor intervened.

There was another time, during one of his heated moments, he knocked me down on the floor, sat on me, and started hitting my chest. This broke a gland in my breast, and I ended up having to go to the hospital for surgery. Because it was my word against his, I was afraid to report what really happened and they just thought I had a bad infection that ruptured the gland, so I needed it removed. Also, it was the early '70s and I felt it would just get worse if I reported it. He worked for law enforcement and often those guys stuck up for each other, and so I felt helpless. I felt that they would probably think I deserved it. At times I felt I did!

He brought the kids up to see me and I had to bite my tongue because they were both filthy and coming to see me in a sterile hospital with dirt all over them. When I ask them to go wash their hands before touching me, he got mad and yanked them away and said I was being bitchy and took them home with them crying because they wanted to see me.

He would not even go wash them up a bit. I was in a hospital bed, just had surgery and risk of infection was high. He did not seem to care. Another way of the controlling abuse I had been dealing with for years. I really thought he kind of loved me but a lot of the time I felt he just put up with me!

As the years passed, to compensate my feeling unhappy and unloved, I started craving the attention of other men. You would think with a husband that could flare up over anything, I would be fearful of being beaten or killed if he found out.

Most of the time it was just innocent flirtations, but over time It was something I needed to feel like I was noticed and special and none of these men hurt me physically, quite the opposite.

My husband apparently talked to our family doctor about the fact he suspected my wandering ways. The doctor gave me a part-time job of collecting rent from his apartments that he owned, and we hung out together even at his home and I spent time with his family. Over time we got attracted to each other and became more than friends. Being a doctor, he had to watch his reputation and if his wife suspected something was going on, it would destroy his marriage and apparently, I was not worth it.

So, we both backed off and I now was back to trying to survive in a marriage I was not only scared to be in, but did not feel hope for happiness if it went on. I really do not think that my husband knew that the doctor was attracted to me, and because it would have caused the doctor problems, I never told him.

I tried to keep the marriage going with my husband by trying to please him while I remembered others that treated me better, but it was not easy. I felt hopeless and stuck, and, in my mind, it was another form of cruelty in my life!

I took up my music again, playing the guitar and singing for the kids and at family gatherings. I usually sang songs that I wrote and one day submitted my music to a publisher, and we did a demo record. It was pretty costly, and my husband was not happy about it, but I paid for it myself in hopes it would go somewhere. (A little naïve I found out)

Little did I know it would end up being on the radio one day sung by someone else same tune, but some words changed. Unfortunately, I did not have the funds to hire an attorney to sue or even know how to go about it, so I just kept the record I made and played it at home for the family and friends. It was called "My Heart." It was based on the teacher I loved back in high school. (the poem earlier in the story was part of the words to the song)

My husband acted like he did not care about the possible theft of my song just the lost money even though I paid for it myself! However, at least I still have the demo record and play it every now and then. I cared even if he did not!

Also, if I spent time with the neighbors or shopped, he would make an issue if I was not home in time to fix his lunch. The kids were only in school a half day, so the morning was all I had for "me" time.

I started getting bored being home all the time and so I got a part-time job at a store as a model for their clothing and learned how to teach a class so I could help other girls become models.

I felt happy in the job and got the children involved in modeling the children's clothes.

I would do the commentary as they walked the runway. My daughter was so cute and she would walk out with her doll and look back at me so shy, but my son was cocky and really had the audience in the palm of his hand. I felt so proud of them both. It was such a fun time in my life!

This went on for a few years, and then I did something stupid. I decided to take an outfit home that I modeled and did not pay for it and suddenly the cops showed up at our door and I was taken down to the station for shoplifting.

My husband managed to talk to the security guard, and later I found out a deal was made to let me go. I did not know what it was, but then the security guard approached me and said if I slept with him, I would not be charged with anything.

I was not sure if again I was being put in this situation because my husband set this up or if the guy was attracted to me. Anyway, I went to the guy's apartment, did the deed and left and the charges went away. I did not ask my husband if it was his idea or not and I never brought up the subject again and, of course, never went in that store again.

Unfortunately, because I was in a mostly violent marriage, I took out my frustration and anger on the kids at times, when they misbehaved. I was always depressed and wishing I was somewhere else all the time.

I loved my kids but because of my unhappiness, I was up and down on emotions all the time. Either happy and playful with them or so unhappy that there were times, I hate to say, I took my anger toward their father out on them, by yelling and spanking harder than I should have. And because of that I would have them nap for hours so I would not get violent with them.

One-time things were not going right, and my son pushed my buttons, and I grabbed the fish tank and tipped it over on the floor. Both kids were scrambling on the floor trying to save the fish. It scared them, but they got on their knees and got most of them saved and by the time it was all done and cleaned up, my out-of-control anger left.

We got the tank back up and filled it together talking over why it happened and put the fish back, and we decided to keep it from their daddy because they knew what would happen.

Then there were times when we would put on a record and dance around like crazy people. We would laugh and exhaust ourselves with silliness and I felt happy during those times, and I felt the kids did too. Unfortunately, it would trigger a migraine, but in my mind, it was worth it for the joy the kids and I had together! You would never see their dad act like that.

During the summer, I met a nice man who was our mail person, and we became friends. I felt so relaxed around him and eventually he told me he was married and then my husband and I started hanging out with them and started visiting each other's homes to play cards. He had a son and he liked playing with our two kids. Down the road the man and I started having feelings toward each other and he also spoke of divorcing his wife if I would divorce my husband. He told me because of the abuse, I would be able to keep the house and the kids.

So finally, after eleven years of fear and anger, I sought help from my male friend who was aware and was witness of how I was treated. He helped me by finding a place to take the kids and stay until I figured out what to do.

It was somewhere my husband would never find me! My friend was my new interest and we even talked about my getting a divorce and eventually having a life together. Because he was helping me, I did not want to say what I really wanted to do. Which was start a new life without having to answer to anyone and just enjoy having a home and having a good life with my children without anger and hurt. I continued to act like I would consider what he proposed, because he was my only help to hide from the danger of my husband finding me.

I met with an attorney, and he filed a restraining order against my husband and made him pay child support while I lived in the house. He could see the kids if his parents picked them up and brought them back. This went on for weeks until he managed to set up a meeting of the man in my life his wife and me. It turned out that the two of them decided it was best to stay together. My ex-to-be brought up that he would be willing to go to counseling if I would and maybe we could get back together.

Because I was devastated over the fact that the guy, I thought not only was willing to help me out of an abusive relationship was trying to get me back into it. I was at a loss of what to do so out of frustration I decided to give it a try and seek counseling and took him back into the home just before the divorce became final.

For the next two years, things went along good for a while. We went camping and fishing together as a family quite often, but I still felt like I had to watch what I did and what I said and even how I acted around the kids and him. (The past haunted me)

I joined a singing group, called Sweet Adeline's. (Barber Shop singing) I did that for a bit. We had to make our own costumes and we sang and did plays. My sister-in-law helped me join and it was fun for a while. We did a lot of singing and I even wore my wedding gown for one of the acts where I had a solo of singing "I'm getting married in the morning" I saw the kids in the audience, and it made me happy that they could see me having a good time.

Soon after that something triggered the abuse to start up again! It started out as verbal and escalated to physical at times. Not as bad as the early years because I learned how to get out of some of the situations by being submissive. He acted calmer with me when I agreed with him, so I just kept my opinions to myself.

One day before having to go to singing practice, I was out in the backyard burning trash in the burn barrel and at the time bellbottom pants were in style. While keeping track of the fire a bee flew up my pant leg and stung me in the butt cheek. I went running into the house and the kids started laughing until I pulled down my pants and the bee got loose in the house. Now the fear of bees set in!

That night I drove to practice on one butt cheek and told the girls in the group what happened, and some laughed, and some were sympathetic.

I still did not let on what I was living with at home. I felt that no one would understand, and his family would ridicule me for saying bad things about him, which would lead to possible consequences?

Who could I turn to for help? Who would believe me? I felt that no one would, so I was on my own to try to solve this. (HE HID HIS ANGER TOWARD ME WELL!!) around others.

After being knocked around one time I asked if that made him feel more like a man and he said yes and hit me again. (Do not ever do that if you are in that situation.) It escalated from there.

I finally decided to save myself from all the anger, violence, and turmoil. I finally hit my breaking point and decided to go look for a place to live on my own I could not afford taking the kids with me yet. While he was on a hunting trip, I looked for a place to move to. I did not have a job yet and was hoping he would be willing to negotiate about the children later when we met with the attorney.

I found a place to live that understood what I was going through and agreed to waive the rent until I got a job. (God bless him.)

A friend helped me move some of the furniture that was in the house to my apartment. I bought food and took all my clothes over while he was on his hunting trip.

When he got home, he walked in the house holding a rifle and asked me what the hell was going on? I gathered up my strength and prepared for the worst to happen. I told him I was leaving and not taking the kids at this time, and he could file for divorce this time and then we can negotiate regarding the kids and the house was his and everything in it and I did not want to live in fear of him hurting me anymore. I also told him the kids were over at the neighbors' and they knew I was leaving, but they also know I would be back for them after I got a job.

I swallowed hard, waiting for him to raise either his fist or his gun, but neither happened. He calmly said that he was waiting for me to finally realize we were not going to grow old together. So, he put the gun down and said I would hear from an attorney soon. He gave me a very cold stare and watched me leave.

I cried my eyes out all the way to the apartment and when I got there, I felt so alone and still afraid of what might happen. What would people think of me leaving my kids even if it was temporary and of course because of how he acted with me around others they had no idea of the abuse I was going through at home.

I found a job working at a company that made computers. It was the late'70, s and I was doing a lot of keypunching and typing and filing and it was pretty much a job I liked, and it paid well enough for me to finally think about getting an attorney. I had not heard from my husband yet. I told him he needed to file this time, which I soon found out that was a big mistake on my part.

I received the papers from his attorney. It said I was an unfit mother and cheated on him throughout our marriage and he was demanding full custody of the kids.

I found an attorney that was recommended to me and showed him the papers. Now that was a new experience. I felt awkward and unsure of what to do. I was trusting a male attorney to look out for my needs in the divorce. (I did not trust men.) I did not know any women lawyers and I was so tired of waiting for things to get resolved.

During all the divorce meetings and planning of who gets what and how much and how the children would be handled. He accused me of cheating on him multiple times and that I was not fit to take care of the children and did not have the finances to support them because my job did not cover insurance, etc.

So, in the divorce settlement, I got enough to pay rent and keep a car and see the kids on weekends and some holidays, but he only agreed if I gave him full custody of them. Of course, I had mixed feelings about all of it, But as I think back, he made me feel unworthy of everything, so I buckled under the pressure that he was putting on me and agreed to it all.

My job was a very busy one, and I learned a lot about computers and was a great office manager but as time went on, mostly because of my flirtatious manner, my boss tried to work his way into my personal life. I did things above and beyond the job description thinking it would advance me to a higher paying position, and possibly a future with my boss down the road.

Well, that did not pan out. He set me up on a date with a client, which I thought was just to discuss business, but it turned out he was pimping me out for profit. The guy was mean and forced me to have sex with him! I felt helpless and managed to talk my way out of being forced to do it again and I was lucky to get away while he was in the bathroom and cried all the way home wondering how my boss could put me in such a situation.

The next day when I arrived at work, I told my boss about it and he acted like it had to be my idea, as far as he knew the man was a nice guy and he hoped the situation did not jeopardize him signing on with the company. Not one word of sympathy for what I went through at all.

Well, the guy came into the office and totally ignored me as I sat at my desk in plain sight and went into the conference room with my boss, and after a long meeting, he came out and winked at me as he passed like nothing happened. I stared back for a second and then looked away as to not encourage him if he was interested in a second round of the night before.

My boss came out with a smile on his face and under his breath said I did good apparently because the man signed up with the company. Then he walked away like what had happened was normal. He gave the impression that he did not feel he had set me up. I wanted to walk out at that very moment, but then I decided to stay on for a bit and kept my eyes and ears open for any other suspicious activities.

I took a business trip with my boss, again testing the waters (so to speak), and caught him shooting up in the bathroom. He claimed he was a diabetic and, since I knew he had some health issues, I did not question it.

We slept in the same hotel room but in separate beds, in my mind I thought he was setting me up with another client, but to my surprise that did not happen and then I thought he had me there to make an attempt to have sex with me instead, but thankfully that did not happen either! In my mind I thought because of his elder years he could not without a blue pill anyway, so I started to relax a bit. I got through the night and next day, it was back to the office and business as usual.

The business had its own attorney and on the sly (trying to get information about the company) I made friends with him, and he asked me out on a date. He owned a motorcycle and when he showed up at my apartment, I was a little scared to go on it with him, but I went anyway, and the evening turned out okay, but I did not get any information that would help me figure out what went on behind the scenes when I was not at work, and he did not tell me anything that would help me find what I was looking for. So, when he asked for a second date, I told him I had other plans with the kids. I never informed him about my kids before and must have scared him off because he never asked me out again.

Another time he sent me out on a delivery in his pink Cadillac and I was to give a briefcase to a man in a medical building. Not sure if it was a doctor or not. Because of my suspicions, I peeked at what was in the case and to my surprise it was full of money. There was no explanation note inside just money. I went inside the building and handed it over to the person I was told to. As I waited for some kind of receipt, he told me he would call my boss and let him know the deal went through.

So, after that I just kept working and since I was the Office Manager, I made mention that I needed to move things in file cabinets to make room for new things. This took away any suspicion of my searching for evidence of what they were up to. I wanted to really know what I was up against before I gave my notice of leaving the company. I decided to look through files—using yearend time as an excuse and made copies of any documents that looked suspicious. This was because I was suspicious of stuff that went on after how I was treated.

My boss did not seem too unhappy about my decision to leave and did not even ask me why? Then after a few weeks, I found out the place was filing for Chapter 13 and moving to another area and changing the name of the company. Again, the red flags came up, and I continued my search until I left, and then I got the hell out of there.

CHAPTER FOUR

Second Life Change

I found a job selling wigs in the mall. The job was not fun but until I could find something better, I tolerated the always angry "boss lady." I swear she had an evil side because one time she told me to sit on a very prickly brush (that you use to comb your wig with) just because I either said or did something she did not like.

Now that I am a weekend Mom, and I am getting a better relationship with my children. I am no longer the disciplinary person, when they come over, I plan fun stuff to do.

Of course, being from a huge number of relatives, and because only a few knew how I was treated in my marriage—the way all abused wives did: "keep silent"—I was blackballed by most of the family for leaving the kids with their father and not putting up a big fight to keep them—none of their business in the first place—and not making a go of the marriage.

The only people that stood by me were my parents, my siblings, my grandparents, one aunt, and one uncle. All the rest made no effort to keep in contact and at family gatherings were either polite or not talking to me at all unless it was my time to have the children and they were with me.

The apartment I lived in was small with only one bedroom, so when the kids were over, they slept on the sofa. They were still young so there was room for them to do so.

One day while sorting through boxes in the move, the phone rang and then another nightmare started. It was one of my coworkers from my computer job, wondering why I quit. And I told him I was not comfortable working there, plus the business was not doing well, so I had to move on.

He apparently went to my ex-boss because then the next call was from him questioning my comment to the person who called. He seemed angry and had a suspicious tone to his voice, so I told him that I did not like how I was treated, and so I felt I needed to leave. Hopefully that was the end of it.

My ex-husband (who worked for the law enforcement) wondered why I quit such a nice-paying job and went to work for a job that only paid minimum wage. So, I told him my fear of what might have been going on. I had told him in confidence, but later, I found out he told somebody at the division. I will go into more detail later about that.

In the meantime, while living at my apartment, my kids introduced me to a man that was the father of three kids they went to school with. They were trying their matchmaking skills.

This was shortly after I quit my wig job. He owned a laundry business.

I mentioned I quit my job at the mall and why and that I was looking elsewhere for work and that my field was bookkeeping, but I needed work and I was willing to do something else just to be able to keep seeing my kids.

So, he hired me to work in the laundry, where you folded sheets on a big press, folded people's laundry, tagged clothes to be dry cleaned, and made some deliveries to hotels. It was quite the physical job compared to the office work I was used to in past jobs.

It was extremely hot in the cleaners, and I was at a big machine that you folded sheets while standing in front of sliding doors that were open for circulation.

One of the days while working, two officers came up from behind me and the girl I was folding with and asked for me by name, I turned and acknowledged them and asked what was up and they told me who they were and then they demanded I go with them.

I looked at the ladies I was working with and hesitated. The officer said I would be under arrest if I resisted. They would not tell me what it was about until I got in the car.

They drove to the state police station and put me in a room with a couple of plain clothesmen. I ended up answering questions about my past job and they wanted to see any evidence I had regarding the possibility they were running a drug ring and using the computer business as a cover-up.

I gave them my testimony and my evidence with the stipulation that I dd not need to go to court to testify, they would use the recorded testimony instead and that someone would watch my home and my kids home until it was over and no longer in danger. They agreed, but shortly after that I started getting threatening phone calls and had to change my number.

As time went on, the man that owned the cleaning business started showing interest in me. I warned him about what was going on, but it did not seem to scare him away.

So eventually we started dating to the excitement of my kids who tried to set us up in the first place. We would go riding in his convertible a lot, stopped at bars to drink and dance quite often. I was concerned about all the drinking he liked to do but from prior experience I kept my thoughts to myself.

There were times when I had my kids that we would all get together and go to the parks to let them play or go to a bar so they could play games while we drank and talked about ourselves.

It was quite a different type of world than I was used to. I could not drink a lot because of my problem with migraines, so I would usually have one and nurse it all during the date. I kept working at the cleaners. My hours were seven in the morning until about four or five in the evening, sometimes later.

Eventually I got promoted to the dry-cleaning area where you sort people's clothes and tag them, so they don't get lost. It was hot work, and, in the summer, it would be over a hundred degrees with just an open door in front and fans blowing the hot air around.

One time while tagging clothes, there was an incident that happened with one of the customers. A plainclothes officer claimed he had about 400 dollars in one of his suit pockets that he forgot to remove before dropping off his suits. I was accused of keeping it because I checked in his items, but eventually, I was cleared when he found the money later in one of his other suits. I have to say that was a scary moment when it was my word against a detective.

On the job, I worked in shorts and halter tops all the time and you were always sweaty. I have to say I still looked pretty good because I was fit, but to me it was NOT A PRETTY SIGHT!

All the time, the kids kept trying to get us to get married. I was renting a house from his parents, and he bought himself a house so his kids could live with him. I noticed he did not seem to be in any hurry to get married at all, but the kids kept working at him and telling him how much they wanted to be a family with his kids. He never really acted like he was in love with me but eventually he must have thought it was a good idea, so he finally gave in and asked me to marry him!

The wedding was simple, and later I found out he was drunk at the wedding and almost did not show up. Why do I keep getting a slap in the face (with reality) when I want to be happy!

Anyway, even with my disappointment I tried to adjust, and an example of how unromantic he was, he decided it was a good thing to take the kids on our honeymoon. It turned out to be fun, but not at all what I dreamed our first night married would be. I felt our first night as a family should be when he took me to his house and we all were together but because I did not want to cause an issue, I just did what I could to try to make it work!

After the honeymoon I moved into his house. When everyone was there, we had seven people two dogs and a cat to tend to. I wanted a better kitchen, so I gave him some of my settlement money from the divorce to remodel it.

The kids, all slept upstairs, and our bedroom was tiny and right off the kitchen with no door for privacy. Not good for lovemaking like newlyweds nor was it good when I had one of my headaches and I had no place to go to that was quiet so I could sleep it off!

The kids all loved being together, my son was the only boy out of four girls, but he got along just fine with all of them. The backyard was huge, so the dogs and even the cat liked staying out in it most of the day. They all seemed to get along and now with all those animals and five kids it was never boring. Always something going on. Not a lot of time to think about how unhappy I was, and I don't think he was happy either according to his actions around me.

He also took off for rides with his oldest daughter a lot on weekends leaving me to tend to anything that came up at home.

One weekend, during hunting season, my husband surprised me by asking if I would like to go with him on a hunting trip just the two of us. I was not much on hunting but because he made the effort to include me, I decided to try my skills at it.

He got a camper and got me a rifle and we went hunting. I was all dressed in orange clothes and was all pumped up to see if I was any good at this venture.

Well, it was cold, so I got some brandy to try to keep me warm. Big mistake I got a bit drunk, walking around with a gun no less, hollering here dearie-weary, and ended up laying on a branch looking up at a squirrel.

It threw me into a horrendous migraine headache, and I was so sick that night, I thought my head would explode. I was surprised that my husband was sympathetic and let me sleep it off but, in the morning, when he wanted to go out again, I downed a lot of coffee and toast to settle my stomach and ease that head pain. Eventually I agreed to give it another try but without the booze. He kind of laughed and off we went.

We both saw a deer at the same time, and both shot it. He claimed it was he who got the deer, so I just went along with it because the scare caused by my first husband came into mind and with guns in the picture it was better not argue the point.

After we got home, he hung the deer proudly and I took pictures and let him be proud of his catch. Then he sent it out to be dressed and we had deer meat forever, which I found out I did not like. I ate it anyway and seasoned it a lot to try to get the gamey taste out. Shortly after we got home I felt something at the back of my neck and it turned out to be a deer tick. Luckily, I did not get sick from it. At least one thing went right for a change!

We went hunting on one more occasion this time for small game and because I sort of had a good time on the first excursion, even though I drank and felt sick. This time it was just a day adventure.

We got to the spot and climbed out of his pickup and got our guns and started heading for the woods when I heard a loud popping noise and felt my hair move that was sticking out of my cap. I turned and my husband had a sheepish look on his face and said, "Oh my God I am sorry. I thought the safety was on and I went to fling it up over my shoulder and it went off.

In my mind I thought he was trying to get rid of me and leave me in the woods. I wanted to say take me home now, but I just gave a look of suspicion, and we went hunting. We did not get anything that day and I did not say much on the way home.

Another time we took all the kids tobogganing. I sat in the back of the toboggan with three of the kids in front of me and the others went on another. We went down the hill and suddenly hit a bump and I was thrown off and landed my tailbone on a rock.

OMG the pain was unbearable. I told my husband I was hurt, and he acted like I had spoiled the whole day and he took the kids home first and then took me to the hospital, where I found I had fractured my tailbone and ruptured an ovary. I was laid up and could not work at the cleaners for weeks. Of course, this did not go over well with him either.

Now, regarding his family, I did like most of them, also, as time passed, I learned, that most of them drank a lot, and since I did not drink much at all, it made me uncomfortable at times and I felt out of place.

My sister-in-law would drink a lot and then want to go dumpster diving and, of course, I had to go because she wanted me to be the diver. (I guess I was more agile to be able to jump in the bins.)

I really did not want to go along with it. but after doing it, I felt strange and excited all at the same time, especially when I found something worthwhile or food that looked okay except for the expiration date!

She and her husband lived above the cleaners and if I had a migraine while at work, I would go up there to sleep for a bit. While up there, I went in the kitchen for water and there were cockroaches everywhere. After that discovery I quit going up there and just went home when I was sick.

Whenever there were parties or events, drinking was always a must and believe me that family could pack it away. Some were nice when they drank, but some were not. Some fights would break out over stupid stuff or advances would be made on my husband or myself that were inappropriate.

One time, my husband was flirting with the employees at our Christmas Party, and I stepped in, knowing he was drunk, and I did not want him to get in trouble with the person he was messing with and found out it was consensual, and she was not against it at all.

So, being upset, I walked home in a snowstorm, and before he did get home, being tipsy I fell on the front step and broke my front tooth.

Even with the pain, when he got home, I confronted him about what happened at the party, and he denied it. I know he was drunk, so I backed off. I started keeping my eyes open regarding his actions. He saw my split lip and bleeding gums where the tooth was broken and laughed and said you look ugly, so go see the dentist tomorrow and get it fixed. I went to work with a puffed-up lip because it happened on a weekend, so I was stuck with it looking horrible. Finally, I was able to get into the dentist and he had to cap my tooth.

As time went on, our relationship became distant and sometimes, he would go to the bar before coming home. Or come home late after I was in bed already. I pretended to be asleep, figuring I would find out what was going on eventually.

There were times I would go looking for him and of course could not find him. I felt hopeless and stupid for acting like a private eye. I stopped torturing myself because if he was cheating (which I found out he did to his first wife a lot) I would either try to live with it or end it. You know the old saying of "ONCE A CHEATER ALWAYS A CHEATER!"

One weekend, I decided to go away and think about what to do. I felt helpless and because I worked with my husband the choice of leaving him meant no job and again trying to find a new place to live. My self-esteem took a terrible dive to the dark side!

In my depressed feelings and worthless state of mind, I decided to grab the sleeping pills out of the bathroom and threw them into my suitcase along with nightclothes.

I don't know if I was really thinking about suicide or just considering it as a way to end all the helplessness and unhappiness that I felt about another marriage failing. I guess I felt that was my only option at the time if I could not figure what else to do with my life.

When I got to the room I rented, I just sat and watched television for some time and thought about all the stuff I had to deal with. I felt very alone and thought my life was a waste of time. I felt like I was just being used all the time and there was no time for me.

I thought about how the job I had to do every day was very long hours and hard work. I could not keep weight on, because the building at the dry cleaners was so hot! Also, I worked every day except Sunday and that usually involved housework. So, as you can imagine, I started feeling like a slave and with the thoughts that my husband was out at night all the time doing God knows what at the bars or elsewhere, I was beyond feeling lonely.

I called my mom and told her about what was going on and how I felt like ending it all and, of course, she let me down again by saying, "How dare you try to take your life. If you wanted to die, I brought you into this world and I could have ended it for you." What Mother says that to a child no matter how old they are. Again, proof of how my mother felt about me!

Was it me? Would the world be better off without me in it? How would my kids feel if I was not around? All these questions went through my mind over and over. So., I downed the bottle of sleeping pills and lay in bed hoping to just drift off to somewhere peaceful, but then fear set in because I was not getting sleepy at all. I bolted out of bed and went in the bathroom and tried to throw up all the pills. I was glad that a lot did come up and I just sat and cried.

Why was I blaming myself for what somebody else was doing to me?

I was dealing with abuse all over again. This time it was not from being beaten or verbal; it was more of being unappreciated and forced to work under extremely uncomfortable conditions and then there was the betrayal that took away my trust in men totally.

I called my sister and told her I was in town and asked if I could come over for a bit. When I got there, she had questions because I was alone. I confessed to her why I was there alone and told her what was going on in my marriage and how I just couldn't take it anymore. I spent the night talking over everything and what she felt I needed to do and that she had no idea of how my husband was treating me, but she would be there for me.

Because my job was with my husband, I felt trapped in a nowhere life. I would be starting all over again from scratch. I had nothing to fall back on financially because the house was in his name and we had no children between us, and I would be hurting the children because they did stuff with him and liked him, and I would be destroying all of that for them for the sake of my sanity.

Well, the decision was kind of made for me. When I got home from my sister's—he never questioned about why I went anyway—he was in our bed with another woman. It was a coworker and I sort of suspected she was the person that he was meeting when he did his bar runs at night. She looked at me as though confused that I was there at all!

Apparently, she was not told that we were still a married couple and I still lived there. I stood there in shock for a few minutes, looking at the wall that held the shotguns and held back the urge to shoot her and just slammed my fist down on the kitchen counter (remember the bedroom was off the kitchen with no door) and told her if she knew what I was thinking she would waste no time getting out! SHE GOT OUT.

I asked my husband why and he said, "I did not expect you home yet and I was going to tell you eventually about her, but the time had not come up yet to do it."

I forced him to tell me how long and the reason for it. All he said was that I no longer fulfilled his needs and that he had been meeting with this gal for some time now and she was a better fit for him, and his girls liked her better than me, (so they knew about it!) and he was about to ask me for a divorce any way.

I just stood there staring at the guns (AGAIN) on the rack above the bedroom! Then I cleared my thoughts and told him I was tired of his crap and that he had no idea how much I gave of myself to try to make our marriage work and I worked my ass off for him at his cleaners. Why did he not discuss his being so unhappy before so we could try to fix it! And why did he not care about my happiness at all and how this whole thing would affect me and my two children? He had no comment and got in his truck and left.

I slept upstairs with the kids until I could find another job and a place to live, which took a bit more than a month! I decided that he owed me a place to stay until I could get my life together, so I stayed at the house. He could be there, but I insisted that his woman not hang around until I was gone, so he spent a lot of time at her place.

Finally, I was able to quit the job at the laundry and found work elsewhere at a furniture store as a bookkeeper. I filed for divorce on the grounds of adultery but had no pictures or anything to prove it, so the accusation was not allowed, and it turned out to be incompatibility. I spent a lot of time going to visit my sister and spending weekends with her when I did not have the kids. Her husband did not seem to mind me hanging around occasionally during the divorce.

My ex-to-be was eager for me to get out of the house so he could hook up with his new lover and made no qualms about expressing it many times or whenever I was around packing. But because of having no money to speak of yet on account of the fact I just started a job, he agreed to let me stay at the house upstairs until I had a place to go, but it had to be soon because he wanted to start a new life with his new lover. He did not feel right having her move in with me still living there.

Remember I stipulated that earlier, so I was happy he was going along with my request.

The young man that lived next to us saw me out in the yard and we started talking about my situation and he said he would help me when I found a place to move to. Hallelujah, I finally had enough money in my new job as a bookkeeper and after a few days of being trained on what the job what all about, I felt comfortable about accepting the challenge. The gal I was replacing mentioned that she was renting a house that had two bedrooms and the rent was something I could afford. After she moved to her new location, I just took over her lease and started to clean and eventually asked the neighbor that I befriended that lived next door to my would-be ex, to help me move what furniture was mine over there.

I also had a dog and a cat that I had in the first marriage, and they were with me throughout the second marriage too, so they went with me to my new place. Now that I was truly living alone except when the kids were over for their weekend visits, the pets helped me not to feel so lonely.

Thinking back about my dad, he did stop by for coffee to check up on me on weekends, but I always kept my guard up not to encourage it because I wanted to be free of all things for a while.

It took a weekend, and a lot of elbow grease to clean and organize before having to go to work the following Monday morning.

Shortly after the move the divorce was final. I did not get any money out of it just bills which were mostly credit cards that were in my name only.

In my mind I felt I had wasted more than four years of my life with nothing to show for it! And I was upset that I did not get the money back that I put into remodeling the kitchen. I guess in no-fault divorces, it is just cut and dried and done.

I talked with my ex for one last time, but that turned into a confession on his part about how he wanted sex a different way then I was willing to do (backdoor style) and she was willing and that made him want to have her. He did say I was a good wife but just not for him. Oddly enough we had one more round of sex (a moment of weakness or loneliness, I guess). Afterwards he left, and I never saw him or his three girls again.

I felt a little less down about myself after he confessed his obsession! I remembered thinking back early in our marriage that I did find books in his drawer that showed his sexual preference and remembered that I did try it once and told him it was not for me. We had relations but not how he wanted it. I thought he accepted that but found out it was not the case.

I thought he loved me enough that he would forget about it and keep our married life going along, but apparently, he could not get past it over our four years together and sought out someone who was a willing participant in the way he desired and apparently liked it. It saddened me, but also it made me feel less guilty of why our relationship did not last.

Also, I wondered why his kids did not want to keep in touch. I know the older girl never liked me, but the twin girls seemed to. I did not dwell on it but wondered if he told them they could not see me anymore.

I was tired of letting men make me feel like I am a failure and not worth the time to be what I wanted in a man. It always seemed like I had to be what they wanted. I needed to get out of that cycle of life.

CHAPTER FIVE

Breaking Away

The house I rented smelled musty because it was in an area that had been flooded at one time. So, the carpet had to be replaced, but other than that, it was a cute two-bedroom house with a decent-size yard for the kids to play when they came over.

I bought a carpet remnant from the furniture store I worked at and replaced the carpet with the piece and stored the old one in a shed because the landlord said I had to put it back if I moved out.

I had no lawn mower, so I borrowed the neighbor's push mower to keep it cut. It was the kind with no motor, so it was a workout for sure when I mowed.

The kids liked the place and fixed up the room they would sleep in and brought some of their own things from their home with their dad over to my place.

Sometimes when they were with me, I would go visit my dad and stepmom mostly because I wanted them to know my side of the family not just their father's side.

Shortly after moving in, of course something had to go wrong. On the first weekend that the kids stayed over, I had to help my son on his paper route and that meant getting up real early. I tried to wake my daughter to go with, but she did not want to, saying, "I am ten years old, and I can watch after myself for a bit." In my mind I felt she would be safe in a locked house for an hour, or so I thought. I was not comfortable about it, but I decided to give it a try. I locked up the house and off we went. When I returned, I was surprised to see a police car in the drive.

My heart went in my throat as I entered the house. She was standing in the living room holding the cat to her chest and crying. "What on earth happened? Are you all, right?" I blurted out. The officer told me that someone walked in the kitchen door, and they were not sure what he was up to, but according to my daughter, as soon as he saw her, he turned and left. He must have had a key because I know I locked the door after we left. And there was no evidence of a forced entry. Thank God she was not harmed. I never would have forgiven myself if she had.

Unfortunately, her father my first ex-husband was furious with me that I did not make my daughter go with us, but because it was early in the morning and the house was locked, I thought she would be okay. So, anyway my ex was not going to let my son come over if he did the route because he felt I could not be trusted to make her go with us to do the deliveries.

So, I felt bad and said, "No way am I giving up my right to see my son over a newspaper route; we need to figure something out, so I can see him during my allotted time!" He finally agreed to drop him off after his route was done so we could have our time together as planned.

After a few months, my brother came to see where I lived. He was a Navy guy and home on leave, so I told him to come over. Now I was not a heavy pot smoker, but I did have one joint left that a friend had left behind and I asked him if he would like to try it. He had never smoked one before. So, we did, and he got a little silly and it was fun to see his reaction, but of course when he went back to Mom's place, and he told her and her current husband about it, I got a phone call saying how could I subject him to that?

I told her it was all in fun and for her to get over it; after all the crap she put me through, I was done trying to please her. To say the least she got angry, and I did not hear from her for a while, which I did not care if all she wanted to do was put me down.

One evening while sitting in the living room, I saw bees flying around the lampshades. (Remember my fear of bees.) Low and behold they had built a nest in the windowsill. My brother suggested that I put foaming sealant around and I could hear the buzzing and finally after having them trapped for days the noise stopped and no more bees.

Unexpectantly, while watching television, my dog started having a seizure in front of my fish tank. I did not know what was going on, so I picked him up—he weighed fifty pounds—and put him in the car and took him to the vet and found out he had a massive heart attack and had to be put down. I felt sad because I had him for at least fourteen years. So, now it was me and the cat.

Soon after that I found an apartment that was called a garden apartment. Luckily, they allowed cats, but you had to pay a fee to have one. The place was cozy with a big living room and a big bedroom. I created a bed out of a twin bed in the living room that also provided an extra seating area. That is where my daughter would sleep when she was over. Also, the place had a workout room and an above-ground outdoor swimming pool.

My son did not come over often, but when he did my daughter would sleep with me but that happened less and less now that he was a teen and had other stuff he wanted to do with his friends on weekends.

When the kids came over, they loved it and had a blast. Finally, I was the fun parent.

During the week, I was busy with my new job as a bookkeeper and manager for a furniture store. I earned the respect of my coworkers and my bosses by always being available when needed and opening and closing the place when nobody else wanted to. I actually got the title of Office Manager! It was tiring, but I felt needed and proud of the respect I now was getting.

It felt good not to have to answer to any man anymore other than my bosses. I felt lonely at times, but then I would think back to all the stuff I endured when married. I blew off the loneliness and found things to do I liked. So, I took up exercise thanks to a coworker and I got so good at it that I started teaching the classes.

A few years went by, and while doing an exhibition in the mall in town, I noticed I had wet myself during jumping exercises. I went to the doctor and after massive testing, I had to have surgery and they found I had the early stages of ovarian cancer and needed an operation to test how far it had spread. I needed a mild form of chemo, which involved pills and my hair got so thin, I wore wigs for a couple months.

Luckily, the cancer cells had not spread, but unfortunately, they needed to do further surgery because they did not take both ovaries and they did not want me to possibly have that one get cancer down the road. So, this meant I had to have a second surgery.

Before the surgery I reminded the doctor of my allergy to some of the stuff they used to sew me up with dissolved too quickly, but they ignored the notes and did it anyway, which resulted in my hemorrhaging a week or so into healing. It happened while shopping in the store for a camera. My family was coming over for my birthday. A little child came up to me and told me there was a pool of blood by my feet. I did not even feel that I was bleeding.

I got a towel out of my car to sit on and drove myself home and called the kids and told them what was going on and to cancel the party. They called an ambulance and I sat in one of the dining tables chairs and when they got there to take me to the hospital I was soaked with blood and the chair was overflowing with it too.

I remember the ride to the hospital because they had to tie my legs together and when they put the IV in it hurt like hell. Then I think I passed out because the next thing I remember was being in a hospital room and they were giving me blood.

While in the hospital my mother came to visit, and she noticed I had a strange smell coming from me. She looked at my second surgery incision and noticed it was inflamed and smelled. It was New Year's Eve and, of course, my doctor was at a party, but they called him in anyway because of the seriousness of it. He looked at it and said to put me on antibiotics and he was going to leave. Well for once my mom was my advocate-thank God or I found out later that I could have died if the infection became sepsis!

My mom stopped him and told him to take another look. He did and realized it was full of puss and smelled really bad, so the nurses stabbed my incision with surgical scissors and started squeezing the stuff out. It turned out to be a bad staph infection and I had to take a lot of antibiotics and could not leave the hospital for several days. It was a scary time! It sort of changed my attitude toward my mom after that, but it did not heal all the hurt from the past.

Finally, I got better and was able to get back to my job at the furniture store and teaching aerobics.

The gal that worked in the office with me told me that she and her husband were going to open a small gym in a town just outside of where I lived, and she would love it if I would teach aerobics there. Of course, I could not turn that down and they even named the gym after me. I was good at instructing and loved it and had wonderful stamina to teach two classes if needed.

Unfortunately, the couple split up and the gym was closed, but I still taught at a Fitness studio on weekends. My daughter started coming to my classes and even taught with me occasionally. The gym even wrote an article complete with picture of us teaching calling us the mother-daughter duo! I felt proud of what I did and glad she was interested in doing it too!

As time went on and because I still visited my dad and stepmother almost every Sunday, my dad decided to set me up on a date with a guy he knew through his work at the plant where he used to work.

I went out on a couple dates with the guy that my dad had set me up with, but I felt no spark. He was quite a bit older than me and not fit at all (which was important to me since I was) he complained about the fact that I put hairspray on my hair, and it made me look like I had dandruff. So, I tried not to use it when I saw him.

Also, when he showered, he did not use a towel to dry. He laid on the bed and said that it was bad for your skin to dry it off; air dry was best! I finally decided that he was too weird for me, even though he had money. There was no way I could live under his thumb.

My dad was disappointed and told me that this guy could take care of me so I could quite my jobs if I wanted to. I once again had to let him know that I did not need his interference or another man to try to control my life!!

Unfortunately, the guy Dad set me up with thought we should be together, because he started stalking me at work by stopping by with flowers and saying things to me in front of my coworker that was embarrassing. I changed my phone number right away. I told him not to show up at my place of work again.

The threat did not keep him away and finally, I told my bosses about him and the next time he came in one of them intervened and told him if he came around again without buying something, the police would be called. He never stopped by again and because he did not have my new phone number, he never contacted me again. (Thank God I dodged a bad situation for once!)

For a while I kept checking the parking lot at night before I left to make sure he was not out there waiting for me but fortunately that did not happen.

After that fiasco, I started to concentrate on my job and build a career in accounting. So, I decided to continue my college education to become an accountant. I took night classes and worked hard. Some classes were very difficult, but I managed to persevere and got my associate's degree in business management and accounting,

I kept teaching at the fitness studio. It was an ego booster with twenty to thirty women looking to get fit with my help. My son and his buddy came once, and I could hardly concentrate because they were being silly, so I tried not to look at them, but I did laugh at their antics once in a while.

I forgot to mention that when I got back to work again at the furniture store, I was walking around during inventory taking notes and because all the workers had to help with inventory one of the drivers noticed me and came over and whispered, "You lost your butt!" I turned and looked into his eyes and said, "Excuse me?" He smiled and said, "I always admired your figure, and I am sorry you lost part of it during your illness."

He was so cute about it, I laughed and said, "Thank you, I think" and told him I was back to working out now and will most likely get it back and we laughed together. He had such a contagious smile.

Later, after I started feeling better, he asked me out for dinner. He told me he was separated, and a divorce was in the works. I took a mental note that he was considerably younger than me, but I figured what the heck? It is just a friendly meal. So, we went out and we hit it off immediately. We talked about everything even some of the bad stuff, but nothing seemed to scare him off.

We kept our relationship a secret from the others at work and dated on weekends. Going for rides in his convertible and going to car shows where I would wear short-shorts and halter tops. I finally did get my butt back LOL. Being an aerobics instructor, it helped me stay in shape if you did not pig out.

He would stop by my apartment to watch TV with me, and we would kiss, and it started to get a little more serious each time. I worried about our fifteen-year age difference, but he did not. I was in my forties, and he thought I was one hot mama. I was enjoying the attention, because who knew how long it would last as I got older.

I gave in eventually and we became what you would call an item. We spent all our free time at car shows and in the bedroom. He was young and horny and because I had a tight body from teaching aerobics twice a week, I had the stamina to fulfill his fantasies.

Our work relationship was kept separate, and it was not until the company Christmas party that people knew about our connection. We walked into the party arm in arm and boy did we get a few confused and disapproving looks but I tried to ignore them. Shortly after that my daughter and I competed in a Miss Fitness contest. If you won, you would be on a calendar for the next year. Unfortunately, neither of us won. I came in third place out of three girls and one gal was very muscular, I knew I wasn't going to win, but I did not expect to be in third, the judges seemed to like and complemented me. So, I made myself believe it was fixed, but it still was not very good for my ego and I got upset. I did eventually get over it and figured it was a good experience and I really was glad I did it.

My new boyfriend went with me to family gatherings and the family seemed okay with our age difference. My dad and mom even liked him and thought nothing of the age difference or just did not want to say for fear I would not visit them anymore. They probably, (like me) did not think it would last, so enjoy it while it lasted.

After about a year after my daughter graduated, she asked if she could come live with me. She confessed how her dad treated her. Also, how she felt during the divorce. I had no idea that she felt rejected all these years because I did not fight for custody of her. Her dad was not mean to her but had no patience when she had her bad headaches and sometimes made her do different chores around the house thinking they would go away if you got your mind off it.

Well in my experience—and he should remember how bad they were for me when I had them—he should have known better and let her go to bed to sleep it off. Unfortunately, she inherited them from me, like I inherited them from my mother and grandmother. I felt guilty about that too!

Anyway, she asked because she was older now and had a boyfriend. She wanted more freedom and, of course, out of guilt for not taking her with me after the divorce, I agreed with the stipulation that the boyfriend was not to move in with us and she was to help with the rent, since she did have a job. She agreed but asked if he could stay the night occasionally and I agreed because I felt this would help bring us closer.

I found an apartment that was meant for roommates, which meant she had her own door to come and go. Her own bedroom and bathroom and I had mine, and the middle was the living room, kitchen, and balcony.

My boyfriend (remember the young stud I was dating) borrowed the company delivery truck to help me move out of my apartment into the new one. That was quite the adventure. The place was on a second floor with a balcony, and so instead of climbing a bunch of stairs down a long hallway to the apartment we used ropes and hoisted furniture up to the balcony and brought them into the living room. It was a little scary at times, but it all worked out.

It worked out perfect for my daughter because now she was able to date and come and go without disturbing me if I was asleep. Unless she went into the kitchen and made lots of noise (which happened occasionally). Her boyfriend was a nice young man and he hung out there occasionally on weekends.

Shortly after that I had to have another serious surgery and had to stay home from work. I came home with a catheter bag that I had to strap to my leg in order to walk the halls, etc. And I was told to do so; it was not a fun time for me.

This opened a way for the boyfriend to move in almost full time because I needed some looking after and he could help me if I needed it. After work she wanted to make sure I had help so she hung around a lot until I got better. I really liked him, and he was always kind to me and respectful if I needed quiet to sleep and they were in the living room and a few times I would get up and ask them to be a little quieter but not often.

After I got well and was able to go back to work, he hung out even more, but I was gone a lot, so it did not bother me that much.

Things started going under at work and the store had to close and, of course, that meant no job for me. My boss was kind enough to put in a good word for me at an accounting firm and after the store closed, I was able to get a job there and was being trained while helping the store wrap up their business.

During this time, I decided to end it with the young man because the age difference really started to bother me. Shortly after I cut things off with him, I heard he found someone else, so I guess I made a good choice before he started the inevitable cheating on me game.

The bosses moved out of state, and for the summer I worked out of one boss's house to do final delivery setups and the last of the book work. That is when I started working at my new job with the accounting firm. Since they did the store's books, they finalized everything and since I worked there it taught me how to close accounts, which I had no experience at.

I worked in the financial department and the gal that was training me was a nightmare but because I needed this job and all the benefits, I just kept quiet and did the best I could and was glad to go home after. This went on for a few months and I still taught one class a week on Saturdays to keep fit plus it definitely was a stress outlet!

When I started working full time at the firm, I met an interesting computer guy that started coming to my cubicle to chat every now and then. I did not try to give out any vibes that I was interested in anything but my work, but he kept asking if I would go to lunch with him and because we would be coming back to work after, I felt it was innocent enough to agree to.

After a couple lunches and finding him nice to talk to, I agreed to dinner one evening. He was very polite and did not monopolize the conversation and seemed interested in what I had to say. So, we started dating more often.

He met my daughter and her boyfriend, and all seemed right with the world. Little did I know this guy had a dark side both on the sexual side and he drank way too much.

Being the kind of person, I was, I thought I could help him and turn his life into something better by being around him. "Big mistake!" He started verbally abusing me and drinking to the point of blacking out. If I stayed the night, he would aggressively try to have sex with me even if I was sleeping. Once he put me on the floor and went at me in a very rough manner! I was afraid and when he was done, I left and went home.

After that I stayed away from him the best I could since we worked in the same building. He kept at me to try to get back with me, but I shut him down and just to deter him I started seeing one of the CPAs. Finally, he got the message and left me alone.

I only went out with the CPA a couple times. I did not feel like we were a fit. Apparently, he did because he started being critical of my accounting abilities and almost got me fired. Luckily one of the elders in the company liked me and gave me a year to either improve or get another job.

In the meantime, they needed a person to shred documents for recycling and because I could use the money, I jumped at the chance. This meant I stayed after my normal hours and did it in the evenings or on weekends.

I started spending more time at the apartment and noticed my daughter's boyfriend was becoming a permanent fixture now and I felt some things needed to be addressed. I talked to my daughter about it, asking for a little more rent money from her, because what she gave me did not cover three people, and we ended up in a big argument and she decided to look for another place to live.

Of course, I was hurt that she immediately went that route instead of negotiating the price and agreeing to stay a bit longer, she then confessed that she felt it was time for her to branch out on her own anyway.

So, thank God we did not stay mad at each other long and she allowed me to help her move to a new place. It was a cute little house. I stayed all day to help her unpack and we talked about what happened at the apartment and she seemed to understand my dilemma.

I ended up staying the night and it was quite the experience. She had filled the waterbed with chilly water and by the time we went to bed it still was not warm. To say the least we bundled up to sleep on it. Anyway, the long and short of it was we finally made peace about what happened, and our relationship was back to what it should be.

I had to search for another place and found an apartment that I could afford. The complex was made up of one level buildings with four apartments in each one. They did not call them condominiums they called them apartments. Mine was a one-bedroom with a laundry room and the kitchen and dining were in one section with a small living room. The bedroom was the biggest room in the place.

The parking was outside and sometimes finding a decent spot was a battle. This one car always took the first spot even though my apartment was first in the building. It really annoyed me and one day we met and had kind of a heated discussion about who was in the right. Because she was older and had been living there and parking there before I moved in, I finally gave in and let her have the first spot; I took the second. It was not worth making an enemy of a neighbor!

Another time, when my mom came to visit and we had to sleep together, we could not sleep because her television was loud. Apparently, the walls were thin, and her TV butted up against my bedroom wall side. So, I got up and went over to ask her to turn it down. She said she did not realize it was that late and it was so loud. I thanked her and after a few long minutes she either turned it down or off because I could not hear it anymore.

The following day, while I was at work, my mom went over and introduced herself to the neighbor and talked about the problem. While over there she went in and saw how the lady's place was arranged and made a couple suggestions that might help the noise issue. I was annoyed at first that my mother butted in, but that night the noise was a lot less loud, so I kept my thoughts to myself.

After Mom flew back home, I was out in my small garden doing some weeding and the neighbor came out. We talked for quite a while and soon we started going out to dinner together once a week mostly to keep her company. She was a retired teacher and spent a lot of time alone. We talked about a lot of different things and our friendship grew. We were friends for many years until she passed from colon cancer.

As time went on, a restaurant owner came into the accounting firm I worked for, and we struck up a conversation several times. He knew I did not like working tax season because of the long hours and went up to my boss asking what I made and told them he would like to hire me as the bookkeeper for one of his restaurants.

My boss approached me on the subject, and at first, I was not sure if I wanted it because I did the shredding of papers for the whole firm as my second job and I did not want to lose that income. My boss agreed to keep me on doing that job if the restaurants still used the firm for taxes and financials.

It all worked out, and so, after a couple weeks of preparation to distribute all my clients, I went on to my next adventure in life.

Starting the new job was quite the nightmare. The gal I was replacing was not very good at demonstrating what the job was all about. Totally different bookkeeping system and she acted like she did not care what she told me about any of it.

The man that hired me was not around when I started—he was off on a cruise with his wife and my other boss his father-in-law. When he came back, I told him that the gal that was supposed to train me did not do a very good job and he would have to go over what I learned and help me learn it the right way. He was very understanding and apologized for not being there when I started the job.

So, with his further instructions, I finally caught on to how his computer system worked and what my job requirements were, and finally, I could relax and feel more confident in my job change.

My other job was for his father-in-law as his tax accountant, and I did his financials for a bar in another part of the state. I felt comfortable doing both and eventually had an office to myself at his insurance business, so I did not always have to work in a small office near the restaurant's kitchen.

Also, during this time of two jobs, I still had a third job of teaching aerobics in the evening and personal training a friend that worked in the insurance company. So, I had no problem filling up my time while living alone.

As time went by and I started feeling more comfortable in my lifestyle and jobs, I thought about possibly dating again. My mind said no because all the men I had met at parties and stuff were either self-centered or assholes. At least that was the impression I got after talking to them for a few minutes!

My boss at the main restaurant I worked for and I developed a friendship and we talked about almost everything.

He had met my kids and was friends with the gal I personal trained, so I felt at ease around him, and a bit attracted to him even though I knew he was married.

Of course, he told me that his marriage had not been a good one for a few years. I know I should have seen the signals of a cheater, but I was lonely, and he knew it, so one day he approached the idea of us spending some alone time together. I thought about it and told him I did not think it was a good idea and that I did not want to risk losing my job if things went sour.

He said he cared about me too much for that to happen. I still hesitated but told him we could meet and discuss it.

We met at the insurance office. We talked a long time and did some what you would call petting, but I called a halt to going further because he was married and there was no talk of that changing.

He still flirted and acted attentive around me probably in hopes I would give in. He would show up at work and close my door and kiss me and then go back out and get busy and leave me wondering what he was up to. I was so attracted to him it took a lot of control not to lock the office door and go at it.

His wife suspected the attraction because one day when the office door was closed, she came to the door and hollered "You dressed?" before coming in. I did not take it as a funny moment, but he did. I glared at her giving her the impression that I was offended, but I know my face was red!

On another topic of interest, as I mentioned, I still was teaching aerobics and power walking with my friend from work. During our walks she filled me in on her boss and what they went through and since she knew my boss well, she told me some things about him and his marriage—which he had told me was not the greatest—she did confirm it.

One night after work I sat on the floor to clean out the bottom of the television stand. It was on wheels and when I was shoving it back up on the stand the wheels caught on the carpet and the television (the old tube type) fell forward on top of my head. Luckily it did not break but I had all I could do to get it up off my head and back on the stand. My daughter happened to show up and I told her what happened, and she stayed long enough to make sure I was okay.

I felt kind of out of it mentally, but I did go to work the next day. While trying to post on white sheets of paper I kept seeing red spots. So I went to Redi-care, and the weirdest thing happened. Instead of them concentrating on the head injury they saw a bulge in my neck and told me to have my thyroid checked.

So the next day I saw the doctor and he ordered an MRI test and discovered that I had a cyst. Also, blood work showed I needed thyroid medicine. They could not do anything about the cyst, they just started doing MRIs annually to keep an eye on it.

The incident did cause me to have some mild amnesia and the doctor had me take Ginkgo Biloba to help heal and stimulate my brain. It took several months before I remembered certain things. The odd thing was I did remember how to do my job and drive, but not birthdays or occasions or things about my past for quite a while and some things I wish I never remembered!

Also, I had to see an eye specialist because of seeing red when I was trying to post to white paper. Turned out the incident tore my retina and I had to do eye exercises and drops until it healed.

The traumas seemed to continue to keep happening unexpectedly indeed!

After several years of doing three jobs, the accounting firm decided they would have the people that work there do the recycling of documents and without warning let me go. That was a loss of income I did not want. Plus, I was close to my twenty-year bonus, which I did not get because they let me go a month before it was time.

My boss at the time gave me a slight raise to help compensate because they knew I was house hunting and car hunting and because I was depending on all my job incomes, they decided to help. Both my bosses were wonderful but always with a secret agenda I found out as time went on.

I had to give up teaching aerobics because I contracted fibromyalgia and it got to be harder physically for me to keep up both doing aerobics at the gym and personal training my friend. Since the gym was not paying me much to train there, I decided to give that job up. It was difficult enough to go on doing power walking and strength training with my friend, but I kept up the power walking with my friend mostly because I enjoyed our talks and it kept me active!

One Fourth of July, the boss that hired me had me come to his cottage to stay the weekend with family and friends. Since he was my other boss's father-in-law, I knew I would run into him, and we would have to pretend we were not involved. Both wives were there.

There was an awkward moment when it came to eating. I have certain food allergies and when offered something I said I could not have the father-in-law boss got angry and said it was all in my head. I then left the room and ate nothing. His wife told me not to act so mad because it would just make him angrier. She told me to get what I wanted to eat when he wasn't looking and act like I was not upset if I wanted to keep my job!

Soon this boss left for their summer cottage and while jogging on the beach dropped dead! I was shocked because he had a physical just before he left for vacation. He must have known he had issues and did not tell anyone because his wife said he had blocked arteries and it caused a heart attack. He was a private man when it came to himself.

After he passed away, his wife hired me to help close the company that I did the books for. I had nothing but a working relationship with this boss, so there was no awkwardness involved.

The relationship with the boss I had left was awkward! He started acting different with me and kept trying to make my life at work harder by changing things all the time and making my job harder and acted like he did not want me around anymore. I thought he was trying to get me to quit. Because of the vibe I was getting I did go on one interview and told him so. I did not like the job offer so I came back to work and saw he was trying to do my job. At first, I thought he was glad I was looking for another job, but when I told him I decided I was going to stay he seemed happy and stopped being mean. I think when he found out all the different things my job entailed, he did not like it (karma maybe).

He took on a new partner, which happened to be the guy that used to be the kitchen manager. He jumped in and started wanting to make changes and talk the boss into spending money—which being the accountant, I knew we did not have.

I took on some more responsibilities and I did a lot of my work on the computer at home and had a ledger I had to post manually to daily. During that time, I made friends with the lady that delivered our mail, and we chatted a lot about life. At the time I was visiting my grandmother (who was in her nineties) a lot and she was put into a nursing home. The home was just down the road from the restaurant, so visiting was easy.

As time went on, my friend started planning her wedding and she knew I was a good photographer and asked if I would take pictures of their wedding. I got excited about it and said yes. It would be my gift to them! The wedding was outside of her farm home and exceptionally beautiful. I got some great shots and she seemed pleased. She used one for the newspaper announcement I felt proud! The reception was held outside too on what was a gorgeous day!

There was a tent where all the food was, and people lined up to fill their plates. I got in line behind a nice-looking man that had gray hair and a bit of a belly and seemed to be filling his plate quite high. I could not help but make a comment about it.

I said softly near his ear so nobody could hear but him. "Now, there is a man who knows how to fill his plate." He looked at me with a red face and I could not tell if he was either offended by it or embarrassed or thought my remark was dead on. I walked away and sat far away from him, because I felt embarrassed for blurting it out instead of just thinking it.

I wandered around the gardens, and I did not run into him again. I guess I was trying to stay clear of him, but he did stay in my thoughts for some reason.

Time went by and I was still busy with work and spending time with my grandmother. During that time, I constantly ran into my aunt while visiting her and we started meeting together to help her have some fun. Grandma was in her upper nineties now and could not see well or hear well. We always made sure she was at the church service, and she always enjoyed the singing part.

There was one time that we dressed Grandma for the church service and my aunt and I sat behind her and suddenly my aunt noticed that we had put her dress on backward. We laughed between us quietly and wondered if anyone else noticed. She still looked great in her dress with a string of beads down the front. I do not think we ever told her because she would have been totally embarrassed and most likely would not have gone to church again.

Some time passed, and before we knew it, Grandma was ninety-eight, and she expressed at her birthday party that she did not want anymore. She was ready to go home to the Lord. It was not long after that she contracted an infection she could not beat, and she passed peacefully in her sleep.

They notified me and I came to sit by her side until the coroner came. It was the longest wait of my life, and I felt her spirit was there with me and glad that I was there until the others came to finalize her situation. After they took her away it was early morning, and I just could not go home yet so I went for a long walk and cried.

The next day my aunt and I helped clean out her room and helped to make plans with others for her celebration of life. It was too cold to do anything yet, so we had her cremated and planned on a burial when the ground thawed.

Finally, a spring thaw came, and even though it was still chilly, we had an outdoor service for her and placed her ashes in the family plot.

My out-of-town family had me record it and take pictures of who was there and send it to them so they could listen and feel a part of saying goodbye.

For some reason I did not understand, my family that moved away thought I should be the informant person of what was going on. In my mind I could not help but think, *hey, they moved away! If family was that important, why?* I felt very annoyed by that responsibility, but I continued doing it out of respect, I guess.

This at least left me with a best friend, my aunt. As time went by, I would go over to her house after work for coffee and we would talk about everything, and she took care of kids in her home, so often I got to play with them and got to watch them grow up along with her.

We did a lot of reminiscing about the remaining siblings, there always seemed to be something wrong going on and with as big a family that my grandparents had (ten if you remember) you could almost expect some trouble.

I had no quarrels anymore with any of them, but I felt she needed to vent about how they all acted, and I enjoyed listening to all of it. My life was not overly exciting, so listening to other people, family or not, and their dilemmas was okay by me.

Also, I still did personal training with my friend that lived on the other end of town a couple times a week and always had man talk and a lot of laughs. But then on one of our walks, I stepped in a hole and hurt my foot and after I thought it was healed, I noticed it was hard to speed walk on it so I had to give that up.

So that left me with an empty spot in my life to look for something else to fill my free time.

Finally, I got around to looking for a house so I could get out of the apartment life. It took about a year to find one that felt like home, so I got it. My brother happened to be visiting from out of state and was there to help. I was so glad because I had no other volunteers.

The place had a large yard, so there was lots of weeding and mowing to do. My dad had an old lawn mower he brought over and other tools to get me started. The place came with a garage and a shed, so I had plenty of area to store tools and finally a garage to park my car in. I always had to park outside.

The car I had at the time I had bought from my dad, and it was time to get a different one. So now it was car shopping time. It was wintertime, but I felt that would be a good time to buy a car that could handle our cold weather. I found one, so I traded in Dad's car and brought home a brand-new one with only twenty miles on it. .

The car fit in the garage with room to spare for things to store along the walls I was one happy home and new car owner. I was also very aware that job security was really important now being very much in debt.

CHAPTER SIX

Starting over again

As time moved on in my life my kids got married and provided me with grandchildren and great-grandchildren. I spent as much time as I could with them when not working. They filled a lot of my lonely times

I decided to get an answering machine for fun. I would sing and play the guitar and have my cat meow at the end. Everyone thought I was pulling the cat's tail! I would change the theme when holidays came around, such as spooky at Halloween and festive at Christmas time. I found it fun and so did my callers from the messages that people left.

Onc day whilc listcning to my favorite radio station. I heard one of the DJs play my Halloween one! I got all kinds of calls from family and friends saying they were surprised when they heard it when they were listening that day, I wondered who let them know I did that sort of thing. I never did find out who it was! Luckily, the radio did not give out my phone number to the public.

After a couple years that machine stopped working and I could not get another one that I did not have to hold the button down while recording, so I had to stop the singing ones and just did a basic (boring to me) message.

Anyway, the fun was enjoyable to me while it lasted!

A few months after that my mail "lady friend" stopped by to deliver the mail at the restaurant and I decided to ask her if the man that was at her wedding was still available. She said yes, so I felt ready to check out the dating world again. I asked if we could set up a blind date so we could meet again and get to know each other.

The next weekend her husband set up a "let's dig a fishpond" scenario to lure him over to the house.

I got there quite early to wait for him to show up, and several ice teas later, he still had not arrived. I told my friends that after several hours of waiting, I did not think he was coming. My friend's husband kept me there by telling me he would call him and see what happened. It turned out that he went golfing with some brothers in his hometown and came home and fell asleep. He said he would hop in his truck and be right over.

So, I stayed against the feeling that this guy did not live up to his word when plans were made. But then a half hour later he showed up in his little red pickup. As he approached the porch, he noticed me and his face turned red, and he said, "What's this all about? I thought we were digging a pond." But then he grinned at me and said, "You were the photographer at the wedding, weren't you?" I smiled and said, "Yes, and you were the man who knew how to fill a plate." Well, this is a surprise, but I have to say a nice one. Sorry I am dressed so sloppily, but I was expecting some hard labor. He glanced over at his buddy! - no pond today, right?

We all laughed and finally the long-awaited date began!

Our friends (I say that because if you remember the guy was his friend and the gal was mine) decided to walk into town for dinner at a Chinese Restaurant. I normally do not eat at those because of MSG factor, but I tabled it to not ruin the mood of the date. It was a gorgeous day and as we walked, we both filled each other in on some of our past lives and our jobs.

I just remembered later when I asked his first impression of me, he said I was very good-looking, but I talked a lot! I mentioned that so did he, but how do you get to know someone without doing that? He thought about it and then agreed and that he really enjoyed getting know me and how much we had in common.

After we ate and walked back to the house (which was in the country) we sat and chatted for a while. It was getting late, and I hate driving in the dark, so I mentioned I needed to head home (since I had been there for several hours before he arrived) I said that part in my head not aloud so as not to make him feel bad for being so late!

Anyway, after I mentioned that he said it was nice meeting me. Well, there was no mention of any future meetings, so I slipped in a question of whether we should exchange phone numbers or not. He looked surprised (I think because he did not bring it up) and so we put each other's phone numbers in our phones.

I then told him not to call for a couple weeks. He looked at me and said, "Okay, but I would really like to know why? Did I say or do something wrong?"

I told him, "No not at all. It is just that I am an accountant," and it was quarter tax time and financial time, and I would not have time to go out anywhere until that was all finished.

He seemed to understand and then I hopped in my car and left. Well, I got lost trying to find my way back home and drove by the house and I looked (out of curiosity) over and saw them all talking out in the yard and I kept thinking please do not look my way, I would be embarrassed. Luckily, they did not.

I do not have a GPS brain or one in my car, so I was not sure how to get back to my town. I pulled up to a stop sign waiting for someone to come by and thank God someone did. I questioned the driver about which way to my town; they pointed the way and forty-five minutes later, I got back to my town! I was so happy to see my driveway.

Two weeks went by, and I was out in my many gardens weeding and planting when the phone rang in the garage.

I answered hoping it was him and my heart took a little flutter when I heard his voice.

He wanted to take me to a festival in town where lots of music would be playing and maybe do some dancing and of course check out the eating areas. I had a couple chairs we could take, and we had a blast. While dancing (which he did not like to do) he just kept smiling and watching me bounce up and down as I went crazy doing my interpretation of it.

After it was over, he offered to carry both chairs back to his truck and on the way, he nonchalantly mentioned, "By the way, I do not know if your friend told you or not that I am a confirmed bachelor."

I replied, "No problem. I have been a bachelorette for a long time after two bad marriages, so I am not a threat if that is what you're afraid of."

He replied, "I did not mean it that way. I just thought you should know I have been single forever and never married." We both laughed awkwardly and got in the truck, and he took me home, both of us kind of smiling in a good way.

I went about my business doing my job and fixing up the house and gardens I bought before I met him, and a few days went by. I had not heard from him and figured maybe; we did not hit it off after all So I kept myself busy, but down deep I was hoping he would call for a second date.

While at work I received a giant bouquet of flowers from him thanking me for a wonderful time. I called him to thank him for the beautiful flowers and he said he was worried that it would be too much too soon. The bouquet was huge and looked like he bought out the florist. I assured him that it was not because I love surprises and flowers. I also said because I was not known to date much, that I was being questioned a lot by coworkers about who they were from. I giggled and told them it was a secret admirer!

After a day or so, he called and asked me out. We went to a neighborhood bar and restaurant for dinner and listened to a band that he was friends with all the members over the years. Because he did not date much either, I felt like he wanted to show me off. He treated me in a way that made me feel that way, (very special and that he was proud to be with me) so I put forward my best poise and behavior.

It was a wonderful night and he seemed very attentive, and I, of course, wore a dress (which I did not very often) I mostly wore slacks and blouses or sweaters. He was dressed nicely in jeans and a nice button up shirt. (Let the flirting and courting begin.)

He took me home and he came in the house for the first time. I was not sure how to take his remark when he walked into the living room— "Oh you're one of those."

I replied, "Yes, I like a neat and well-decorated home. Is there a problem with that?"

He replied, "Sorry. I was not criticizing. I was just shocked. I'm used to clutter, being a guy, you know!" Even after that explanation, his comment bothered me!

So, my mood was soured for a romantic evening! I suggested we call it a night.

We walked out of the living room, and he stopped and pulled me close to him and gave me a short kiss on the mouth and told me he would call soon and then added if that was all right and I said OKAY as I kind of pushed him out the door.

I don't know why his remark about the house bothered me so much, but it did, and I thought about it for a few days and then I realized he was probably nervous and did not know how to respond to a home that was clean and neat because maybe his family was not like that.

His actions reminded me of my first husband (because he always found fault with me) that I did not answer his phone calls for a while trying to figure out if it was a mistake to go out with him again and just chalk it up to another failed relationship.

A few days went by, and he kept calling me mostly at night. Finally, I answered, and his voice sounded relieved.

He told me he worked until 9:00 p.m. a couple days a week and he just wanted to talk about our last date and how he felt like he had lost any chance with me because of his blurting out stuff without thinking first.

I told him that I had been married to an abusive husband in the past and he always put down anything I did and that when he said what he did a red flag came up.

He wanted to know more about that husband so he would not make the same mistake again. He had never encountered a person who was treated like I was, and he wanted to understand more about how to help me overcome my fears.

I told him I wanted to drop it for now and talk about other stuff. So, we started discussing different topics and some got a little on the kinky side that we both felt a little embarrassed about and quickly changed the subject.

We would talk for over a half an hour before we realized how long we had been chatting about God knows what. So, we would say good night and he would say he hoped he would see me soon.

We made plans to do something that weekends because we both worked weekdays a lot and we happened to have that weekend off at the same time.

Our next date was on a fishing trip. I told him I liked to fish, so we decided to give it a try. It was kind of funny because he acted awkward and surprised about how I seemed to enjoy something he did not think girls liked doing. I explained to him that I grew up fishing and putting a worm on a hook did not bother me and having to go pee in the bushes did not bother me either. He seemed to enjoy my enthusiasm and he smiled a lot.

Afterwards he would take me home, he kept hinting that he wanted to stay the night and I kept putting him off.

I did not want our relationship to go that far yet because in past relationships it just seemed to be an issue and eventually, I would end it because of how I felt about it. More about that later.

Sometimes I would go to his apartment after I got off work and before he got home and make us dinner and we would watch TV together and snuggle. One thing led to another, and we started seriously kissing and he suddenly wanted to see how far it would go. At the time I did not know he had an issue in the lovemaking department until we started getting it on, but unfortunately, he could not follow through.

The rest of that evening was a bit tense, but I tried not to make a big issue about it, so we just watched a program on television and snuggled on the sofa a bit and then I went home.

I stayed away for a bit because he acted like he was uncomfortable around me, and I felt awkward and not sure how to deal with his problem.

Eventually, I called him and told him we needed to talk about the problem and see if we could come up with some sort of solution. We sat and talked for hours, and he explained how he was hooked on watching porn movies and masturbating to them because he had no one in his life to make love to.

Well, now he wants to correct that, and he said he got rid of all the movies, and he wanted to try again with me to see if he can overcome his mindset about sex.

Well, of course I thought because I was very experienced in that department, I could help him. So, we tried different things to have relations the usual way, but he just could not finish without masturbating. I felt like it must be me and I did not turn him on, and I almost stopped seeing him because of it.

I must confess some of the things he would do to me while pleasing himself was, kind of a turn-on for me. I was still not totally comfortable with how he had to have sex with me that way so I suggested a therapist to find out if this could be resolved so we could have intercourse and not feel like we were doing a porn movie version.

He agreed to talk to a professional because he did not want me to give up on him and what our relationship could become in the future.

So, I continued to go on dates with him and mostly I really enjoyed our time together and we continued trying to have relations, but it always seemed to fail. I continued to be patient and told him. "Let's table it for a while and just hang out together like we were just best friends." He did not totally like the idea, but he went along with it.

So, we went out to dinner often and went fishing a lot and went for car rides in the country, which we both liked doing.

One day on one of our fishing trips, I packed a lunch and while sitting at a picnic table eating the lunch, he looked over at me and said the L-word. I did not say it back, but I did say something like "are you sure?" because there were still issues to be resolved. He said he had never felt like what he feels with me with anyone else and he just felt like saying it to me.

A big smile crossed his face and I smiled back but still did not return the feeling. Still not sure in my mind if I wanted to commit to that statement yet.

He came over to the house often and we would watch television together often snuggling on the sofa together and even laying down being silly by swapping a breath mint back and forth while kissing.

He would continually ask if he could stay the night but because, (as I have mentioned before) of past issues with men only wanting me for sex and then moving on when something better came along,

I told him that I was holding out for a permanent relationship (like marriage) before I would let any man move in. He respected what I said after I explained why, and he stopped pushing the issue, but kept giving little hints in the way he acted before I made him go home after an evening together.

Time went by and around Christmas I was invited to a party and I invited him to go with me, I wanted him to meet some of my coworkers and friends. I bought a dress and got my hair done and when he walked in, he had that wow look on his face, so I knew I looked good. He had on a nice dress shirt and slacks and looked very handsome. He said he wanted to talk about something before we left for the party.

So, we went into the living room. I did not want to sit in the dress yet, so I stood in front of him and asked him what was up. He started saying how much he cared about me and wanted to have a life with me and pulled out a box with a ring in it and asked me to marry him!

I thought for a minute and still thinking there might be hope for a normal relationship eventually I finally (but in my mind with reservations) said yes.

We went to the party and told a few people and suddenly we were the center of attention and people were taking our picture and making a lot of nice comments about how we made a cute couple, and the ring was beautiful.

Because it was Christmastime, we had a double date with my daughter and my granddaughter went along, which was kind of cute.

My daughter could tell something was up because my guy was red-faced and acting fidgety. My granddaughter said, "What's up Grandma?" We both looked at her and I held out my hand with the ring on it and they all said, "We knew it!" and the night was one of joy.

Unfortunately, I was allergic to gold, and we had to go and exchange the ring to silver. This turned out to be a good thing because while at the jewelers we were lucky in exchanging we could get a diamond that had two matching wedding bands with diamonds. After he picked up the new ring, he came to the house and actually got down on one knee and said let me do this the right way this time, and proposed again. It was so sweet and now I actually felted engaged.

Now to plan the wedding! He wanted me to pick the day. So, I decided on a spring wedding. I made most of the arrangements because he really had no clue what to do. I asked my daughter to help.

We went looking for wedding dresses, which turned out to be a fiasco. The people were rude to us, and I could not find anything I liked!

I ended up going to different places by myself. and bought two outfits that I cut up and made into my wedding dress. I had to sew it all by hand because I did not have a sewing machine and I got it done just in the nick of time!

My friend the mail lady who was very pregnant at the time was my matron of honor and my fiancé had had his best buddy that he had known for years be his best man and his wife was the photographer.

Of course, I had my fiancé help with some things like the table arrangements that would be gifts for our wedding guest. I felt he need to feel part of the plans.

We decided on the courthouse where we could have a room for people to be a part of it. Our magistrate was wonderful and gave us lots of time. Lots of pictures were taken and we even drove around town honking horns until we arrived at our reception, which was at the restaurant I worked at.

It was all very special, the usual toasting and candor and their choice of food on the menu and drinks on us and it seemed like everyone had a great time.

As a wedding gift, the boss gave us a discount on the tab. It was not as much as I had seen him give others, awkwardly I did mention it to him and kind of in a snotty way he just said he thought it was fair. So, rather than have an issue at work I decided to drop it.

After we left, we went barhopping and boy did I get drunk, mostly because I wanted to loosen up and turn off my mind! Unfortunately, I still had doubts that getting married was the right thing to do, but I really loved this man and wanted it to work no matter what! I was hoping now that we were married his mindset about sex would change.

He reserved a hotel room for our wedding night, but I kind of spoiled the first night by having a terrible hangover from all the drinking after the wedding. So that night I lay in bed snuggled up to him while he watched sports on television.

By the next day, I was better, and we went back to my house to feed the fish and check on my cat. Then back to the hotel to finish our honeymoon weekend.

The Monday after the weekend, we both went back to work. Eventually we started planning our real honeymoon trip for at least a week.

We finally had time to take a week off work and flew to the state my brother lived in.

I asked my kids to come over to the house and feed the cat and the fish and water plants while we were gone.

To my surprise my husband hired some guys to come over and put a new roof on the house while we were gone. The head guy was a brother of one of his bosses and apparently had a fixing-up contracting business and was apparently trustworthy enough to do this unsupervised by us.

I let my husband know that I did not appreciate him not discussing this with me before he made the decision to go through with it. The house was mine before we met and although I appreciated him having it done I did not like being left out of the decision-making!

He apologized and said because I had a carport built for him before we got married, he wanted to do something to improve the home too so he would feel more like the home was his too. We both smiled and all was good between us.

Back to the honeymoon: once we got to our destination, we found out they had all chipped in and got us an apartment so we could spend alone time for our honeymoon phase! It was a nice place and strangely me being allergic to chocolate it was above a fudge store. Since we came and went a lot, we never found it open. Later we found out it was off season in this little town and so they were not even around.

We tried sleeping together, but he snored so loud, and he refused to cooperate about it (like roll over or go to the sofa so I could sleep) so I got up and went to the sofa instead to sleep. He just did not understand why it was an issue. Apparently, snorers don't hear themselves.

Well, that put a damper on a romantic honeymoon, but I kept up appearances around the family and acted like we were having a wonderful time and being the lovebugs they thought we should be.

I tried hard to fire up our sex life by being submissive on whatever her wanted to do, but inside I felt a bit trapped on what to do to straighten the situation out and be happier that I went through with the marriage.

Finally, I just decided it was not worth losing my best friend over, so I just kept doing what he wanted in that department and pleased myself when he was not around. I felt my life was doomed to always be the one that gives in.

Well, time went by, and we both worked a lot and tried to connect on weekends, mostly with my lead. I still wanted to keep trying rather than go without altogether. I had needs and having whatever attention I could get in that department from my husband was what I was settling for. I did not want to go the cheating route. I really wanted us to be together no matter what. I worked hard at it and eventually he tried to be the husband I needed.

My husband's parents seemed to like me, and we would go visit a lot. Suddenly his father got another form of cancer and was dying so we went to his hometown on several visits until finally he was put in the hospital where he eventually passed on.

Shortly after that I heard that my mother had a stroke and things did not look good, so I flew out to the state where my brother lived to see her, and my sister also was there.

I told you in my childhood chapter that I felt like I was an outsider when it came to the two of them. Well, I still had that feeling when I was forced to sleep on a sofa while my sister slept on a fluffy bed with her own bathroom because she got there first. That may sound petty but it kind of hurt my feelings to be treated like the outsider again. I hope it was not intentional but to this day it bothers me.

I no more than got home and got a phone call that mom had died. So, my husband and I booked a plane and again the (outsider situation) we ended up sleeping in the RV! While my sister again had the fluffy bed with a private bath. Again, she said it was because she got there first! Even my husband did not understand that scenario, but we just went along with it and had to walk from the RV to the house to shower and either dress in the bathroom or throw on a robe and go back to the RV to dress. It was all I could do not to lose it, but my mom's death was more important than my treatment while there.

After the funeral, we went back and we both kind of shook our heads about the whole thing and we for some reason (don't know if it was how we were treated or not) we just never went back there again. We thought about it but it never seemed to happen.

Once we got back, we started to hear that my husband's mom was not doing so well. So, we made a visit and found out her heart was starting to fail.

One of his brothers was living with her, and even though he was not doing well either, he did keep us posted and finally we had to go visit and try to convince her to have the surgery she needed, and she just would not budge. After some time and her refusing to have the operation, they wanted to do she died in her sleep.

This was when I had to start keeping track of my dad and step-mother more closely. She was in her eighties and Dad had just turned ninety. They stilled lived in their home and seemed to be functioning okay but still after losing both my mother and my husband's father not too far apart from each other, it seemed more important to keep better track of the parents we had left in our lives.

I kept working and trying to plan different things to do and trying to get my husband to do stuff with me family-wise and spend time with friends.

He was having difficulty dealing with his mom's passing because suddenly he had to help handle her estate stuff and he found out neither parent had a will. I stayed out of it because he as much as told me to.

He got really quiet and kept to himself a lot after his mom passed and I felt other than being there for him I needed to give him space.

The stress of it all made him come down with a flu bug and he decided to sleep in the guest room. I guess we both found out we could sleep better apart, and it became a permanent thing. On the humorous side we made appointments to meet for intimacy. (He got better at it during that time.) Must have turned him on!

When I would see him watching other women or what looked like flirting in front of me—I had trouble trusting him because of my issues in my second marriage and I tried not to show it, but I did accuse him a few times.

This all came on when we started not sleeping together. It bothered me and caused me to doubt his faithfulness to me at times. Like an idiot I would blurt out my suspicions at times and he would get furious with me but never really denied it. He would just say you need to trust me! I am not your ex!

This started to eat at me, and I constantly wondered where he went when he would go away out of the blue by himself and not come back sometimes for hours. I questioned him and he would always say window shopping for tools or just riding around and "listening to his CDs."

What was I to do but believe him if we were going to stay together? I did not want my third marriage to be a failure and I was sure at our ages (now in our sixties) he wanted his first to work out too. So, I just kept a lot of my "unsure about life" feelings to myself.

Eventually he did not attempt to have relations with me at all. I started to worry if it was me, if he was not attracted to me anymore or what? This went on for a several weeks. I finally asked him if that was the case, and he told me he blamed it on his new meds for blood pressure and cholesterol. The times of intimacy together began to dwindle, and so I once said (and I wish I hadn't) that I felt like we were just roommates now. Of course, he felt hurt by that, but he also understood that our closeness had gone downhill, and he felt he could not do anything about it and said he would work at being a better husband and try to make up for it in other ways. Well, I felt hurt that after all the years we had been married he had to WORK on being a husband?!

While at work the boss set up a computer system that I could do the statements on and do banking stuff and, I was able to access my personal email. My husband and I would pass notes (so to speak) while at work and sometimes it was good and sometimes, we would argue through our emails.

I spent a lot of time in my office because I did not like how my boss and his partner acted like they wished I would just quit and leave. I did not know why until later when my boss's wife told me that they were trying to sell the place and probably were trying to get me to look for a job elsewhere in my best interest.

I went in and asked them both "What could I do to help keep us going without my quitting? So, I told them I would reduce my wage and because I was already sixty-two years old, I could get social security benefits and still work for them. I would just cut my hours some to not feel taken advantage of. They agreed to give it a try and they also were cutting their income too. At least this could keep us going until a buyer came along.

This went on and I found I had to do a lot of creative bookkeeping decisions and we had lots of meetings to keep us on track and eventually a buyer came through. Now it was the meeting that all employers and employee's dread—the "we are closing" talk. First it was the talk between the managers and then it was the whole group together. It went well and everyone wished each other the best.

Now, it was time to sell off equipment and clean the place out. I worked at the office most of the time, but sometimes I took work home and did it there to avoid all the tearing down racket. Eventually they brought all the office stuff that I needed to my house, and I worked there on stuff until the closing statements were finalized.

This took a few months and during that time I was not getting a paycheck, so I was collecting unemployment, which I had never ever had to do before in my life.

I still had to help a bit after all was said and done, with closing the company on the computer I brought home that held all their information until a couple years passed. and then I did not have to do anymore work for them.

Eventually, I had to look for a job to please the unemployment agency and started working for a card store. It was only part time. So, finances were very tight at home. Hubby was still working his full-time job, but down the road and out of the blue he got laid off.

I was grocery shopping and he called and told me over the phone to limit my spending because he was let go at work and heading home. I stood in the aisle in disbelief for a bit; then, as usual, just accepted the issue and checked out and went home to find out what happened.

Apparently, the employees complained about his temper and critical attitude about how they were standing around on their phones and not doing their jobs and some threatened to quit.

Well, of course, the boss believed them and did not even ask my husband his side and did not really give him a reason for asking him to leave. Then we heard that he had a younger guy lined up for the job and decided to hire him and it happened immediately.

At least that is what my husband was told by a coworker, and I had no reason to doubt him. Now he was also on unemployment, so it was "tighten the belt" time for real this time.

We went on with me working part time and on unemployment. He started doing the house chores now since he was home all the time now for a few months or so and then he decided to look for part-time work. He did not like being home all the time and I really could not blame him.

During this time, my husband had to have some major surgery and it was touch-and-go for a bit, but, THANK GOD, he made it through and after a few weeks of healing he was able to look for work.

He started a driving job with dealerships. He loved driving, so it was right up his alley.

Now we were really not connecting very much because he drove all day and I worked nights. So, I would come home and spend some time with him watching television and then go to bed. You would think that would drive us further apart but actually we started enjoying each other more when we did have time to spend together.

During this transition in our lives my stepmother was hospitalized with a broken leg. She was already in her eighties and when they sent her to rehab, she started bleeding internally and now she was on death's door.

My poor father was beside himself, being ninety-two at the time, he was totally at a loss of what to do and so I jumped in to help him try to understand and realize how serious this all was. Of course, I did not know at the time that he had early dementia issues and his memory was not as sharp anymore.

After she passed, the stepdaughters decided to descend upon Dad in his home to clean out her bedroom and I decided they were not going to do it without me being there to protect Dad's interests and hopefully keep him from being upset about the intrusion of his home.

The girls tore the place apart in her room and it was a mess. It turned out that my stepmom was a hoarder of shoes and clothes, so donations donations donations happened.

One disturbing thing happened. I found a note tucked in the jewelry box that instructed the girls to look under the mattress. Well, out of respect, I decided to do it and found money hidden there with a note that said, "for you." The girls naturally assumed it meant for them, and not the step-children, but I insisted that Dad know about it, so I showed him the note and he said to just give it to them and so that was that.

I helped set up the funeral with my stepmother's kids and they had the gall to suggest she be buried in the grave with their father, her ex-husband, and Dad went along with it. I was totally surprised but again not surprised because of Dad's mental state. Found out later that he wanted to be buried in his mother's grave and had already made the plans.

A few months passed and I would spend as much time with Dad as I could either before work or on my day off to make sure he was doing okay and not hurting himself! With him being alone now I was not sure about his safety or his mental state!

I continued to work part time at the card store and then looked after Dad on my days off or before I had to go in. He was starting to not be clear in his mind and it became worrisome!

When Dad was turning ninety-three, I decided to have a party at his house and my brother and sister came to stay with him during that time. A lot of family on all sides came and Dad got really emotional, but I was glad we did it because that was the last gathering at his house.

Before my siblings left to go back to the state they lived in we had a family meeting (just us) and decided that if Dad got worse mentally it was okay if I needed to put him somewhere where he could be watched twenty-four-seven. I became his power of attorney and for a year he seemed settled, and I was there every day to tend to his needs until he started getting a little violent when things did not go his way.

Eventually, after discussing it with my brother and sister who both lived in another state, I suggested becoming Dad's power of attorney over everything to help handle things he could no longer handle.

There were times I would stop by to check on him or just stay to do his laundry, fix lunch, or whatever and my son would stop by and visit too. Dad confessed he would still think that his wife was around at times, but he knew she wasn't, but he liked to think she was. It gave him comfort.

There were a few times he fell, and I had to leave work to take him to either the doctor or hospital and this started wearing on me. So, I ended up getting him a medical alert machine and he wore a bracelet that he would push a button if he needed help. It was too tricky for me so my son came over and set it up.

I felt a little better leaving him alone with that as a backup but as time went on, it seemed more like a game to him (he would push the main button to hear it say thank you) crazy but funny too when I saw him do it.

After becoming power of attorney over everything, I started paying his bills and started stopping him from constantly wanting to go to the ATM machine when I found his money was not as much as he thought it was. He got angry with me when I took his card away, but finally, after I showed him his bank statements, he backed off and accepted that me just giving him spending money was more reasonable than him withdrawing money almost every day at the machine.

My dad was also very sneaky when I was not around and would ask my son to do things in the gardens or the yard that I knew would be a good selling point, but my son did whatever Grandpa asked.

One time I got after my son for not remembering that I oversaw my dad, and he needed to go through me on things that needed to be done. He started mouthing off at me (later I wished I hadn't) but I lightly slapped his cheek and I said, "You don't talk to your mother like that,", and he lost his temper and got a little rough physically with me. My dad heard the commotion upstairs and he came up and I told him what happened, and he told my son that he had better leave.

I was so upset that I would not stop by the house if my son's car was there. I felt a little unsure of how to act around him, because it made me remember how his father was to me all through our marriage and the look on my son's face was just like his father's was when he was angry and for the first time I was afraid of my son. What an awful feeling! I prayed a lot about how to get past it!

When I told my husband what happened, he did not know what to say and my daughter said it was my fault it happened because I hit him first. That was hurtful also.

Anyway eventually, I got over the fear because I needed to be there for Dad, and I could not let one bad incident deter me from doing my duty as his caregiver.

Time went by and Dad realized he was not happy being in that house alone anymore and felt he was ready for what was inevitable. I told him for financial reasons we would eventually have to sell the house to pay for him staying in the new place.

Dad fought the idea of selling the house and going somewhere else, but eventually and to my surprise, he went along with it and we made the appointment. After spending a considerable amount of time searching for a place he liked, we finally found one.

It was amazing how expensive assisted living places are! Because I was doing all of this before the house was sold, I had to help a bit on the financial end of it.

Now because I was considered Dad's caregiver, a friend of mine suggested I go see if the Veteran Association could help financially and luckily because of Dad being a World War II veteran, he qualified for some financial aid. That really lifted a burden for me.

After Dad moved into his new place, I really enjoyed my time hanging out with him and made friends with some of the other people who lived there. I would try to be there when some of the activities were going. I felt comfortable leaving Dad in the place because he was being watched and he seemed to like it a lot when I observed him on my visits.

My husband would come over and keep him company on the days I had to work if he did not have to, and since Dad could leave the place with people (he just had to sign out and in) they would do guy stuff. My dad really enjoyed the company of men more than women because I knew he did not have great respect for the females. but I ignored it.

There was a time when Dad acted like he did not like being there and kept asking me if that is where he was going to be until he died. I kept having to remind him that he needed the looking after that I could not provide, so this was now his home for now and I was in no hurry for him to die. After making friends, he seemed to be in better spirits.

I talked to a realtor to find out what I needed to do to sell the house and one of the things was to have an estate sale to clean the house out before selling.

Now that was an experience. Some people walked off with stuff that I did not want to sell. The company handling the sale had to replace the items.

After the sale the guy I hired to sell the house kept telling me stuff I should do to make it more appealing to the client and so it was hire someone to paint the inside and someone to recheck the wiring, etc., etc.

After all that the person that did buy it said I did not have to do any of that because he was a contractor and actually paid me back for the cost of the paint job because he was going to redo it. Wow, that really surprised me. But unfortunately, I ended up selling the house for a lot less than I originally asked for, but now it was done.

When I told Dad that the house was sold, he seemed like he did not know why and so I had to remind him of the fact that he was living in his new place so this will cover the cost of it. He then asked who bought it, and I told him that a couple from down South who were in their seventies bought it and their son and grandchild were going to move in with them. They had nothing but compliments about how the house looked. He thought about it and just seemed to accept it. It was hard to tell, but he never brought it up again.

I tried to visit often and enjoyed helping others if they needed it. On a day I was not there, from what I was told Dad fell in one of his girlfriends' bathrooms and had to be taken to the hospital. It turned out he hurt his back and had to go to physical therapy.

They put him in a facility, which he hated because he told me they were rough with him. I went to visit deliberately during his rehab time and saw how they were pushing him when he was crying with pain. I stopped the therapist in his tracks and told him that Dad was going on ninety-five and this was ridiculous to treat him so rough. He argued with me, and I reported him. The next day I got a call that Dad had broken his hip and was in the hospital again.

Well, that did not go well, as you can imagine. Dad had surgery, which at his age I was surprised he survived and now was stuck in a wheelchair. He was in tremendous pain and because of his now-advanced dementia he did not understand why he hurt so bad and why he could not walk! I felt helpless watching him cry from pain.

When they released him from the hospital, they decided he needed to go to what was called a Memory Care Facility. That was the most devasting thing I had to do. I watched him slowly give up on life and when I would go visit, he acted like he did not care about anything, He often said he was ready to go and hoped the Lord would take him soon. That was so hard for me to hear but because of his pain I understood his thinking. Eventually he was put on Hospice because he was starting to waste away and in a lot of pain!

Well, one night he got his wish and had a stroke that took him. The people that worked there told me he was throwing kisses and saying goodbye to everyone during the day and that that night they found him in bed with a smile on his face as though he saw an angel to take him to his heavenly home, as he had his stroke.

The one thing that really helped in the grieving process was that he had his funeral all planned and mostly paid for. So, we followed his lead and I decided to have the Honor Guards ceremony and let my brother take the flag home.

Now, my parents are gone, and my husband's parents are gone so this makes it even more important to keep our connection with each other our priority.

After Dad's passing, I felt a hole in my world. I had started enjoying all the time I was looking after him and because my husband was gone a lot it filled a void in my days.

I know my husband missed my dad too but in a different way. I think he felt my dad was more of a burden to me than anything else, but it was not true. My dad and I talked a lot about his past and any other topic he wanted, and I learned a lot about what made him tick and to this day I miss the closeness we made over time. (The unpleasant past with him while growing up was forgiven and buried.)

Unfortunately, shortly after dad's funeral, my husband had to have an eye operation that made him half to look down for two weeks. I got him lots of audiobooks to listen too while I was at work. It was quite uncomfortable for him, but after it was over, he got almost all his sight back. He missed quite a bit of work and, of course, was anxious to get back to it.

He did finally get back to driving and I kept working at the card store and all was going okay, and I enjoyed the distraction from my loss, but then a new manager came in to take over because the other one had to stay home to look after her mother.

Well, the new manager was not sympathetic to my health issues at all and started making me do things that hurt me.

One day I came home and told my husband about it because he would constantly hear me complain about how I was treated, and he suggested I just quit. So, I gave him a note that said I was done with her abuse and the key for him to take to her. She called and said, "I did nothing wrong" several times and as you know when people keep repeating the same thing, there is a guilt factor involved.

I kick myself for not going to unemployment and complaining about her, but I had no solid proof other than other employees witnessing it and they did not want to jeopardize their jobs, so I let it go. I felt God wanted me to forgive and forget things that happen to me again.

I was still hurting over my dad and not feeling good about how I quit. But what was done is done; there was no going back!

Because I started getting bored at home, I decided to try working on crafts to pass the time. Now a pandemic was going on, so I was staying at home for the most part anyway. After a while, the crafts filled many containers and still the craft shows were not opening yet.

My husband kept doing his driving jobs and seemed to enjoy being away from the house and it started to feel like he just did not want to be home with me.

Now it was summertime, so I had lots of yard work to do (which I really enjoy doing). I also helped a neighbor out with his. He had a bad back and bad knees, so yard work and keeping house was hard for him, so I told him for a small fee I would come over once a week and do his housework.

At first my husband did not like the idea, but I told him I needed an outlet away from the house like him and his driving job, and then he shut up about it.

After a while he started talking to the neighbor I was helping, and they became friends over the fence and sometimes he would wander over to his garage for man talk.

One time while cleaning over at the neighbor's house his beautiful blond Pitbull that loved me, and we would play a lot when I was over there, jumped up and her full weight stepped on the top of my foot and tore the metatarsal muscle and I had to walk in a boot for a few weeks. It was the time of year for yard chores so I created a baggie to fit over the boot so I could still do some of it. I am not one to sit and just do nothing, I love to keep busy!

Another example of things that seem to happen to me was when a dog I had played with frequently tore the skin off the top of my hand when we were both reaching for her toy. Luckily, she was fully vaccinated, and I did not have to have rabies shots, but it took weeks for the skin to reattach and fully heal and I had to down a lot of antibiotics to ward off infection.

Every time I said goodbye to my husband when he left for his driving job, I worried he would get in an accident while driving but luckily that did not happen.

Sometimes he would be gone from early morning to late at night, but he seemed to like doing it and I just kept wondering why he could not retire with me and stay at home and do some stuff together.

To this day I do not have the answer other than he said that he did not have hobbies like I did. He talked about getting one like building birdhouses, so he bought the equipment in the hope to start, but until then, he explained that he would get bored and had to get out of the house.

But the thing that bothered me was that on some of his trips I could have gone along, but he would not invite me to go along. I asked why and he always said he liked the time to himself. I did question him about that, and he just acted like he thought I liked my time to myself too. Yes, I did but not every day!

He did not seem to get my point, so I just dropped it and let him do his thing and I did mine. It was not worth a fight.

He was a bit overweight, and was on a lot of meds for cholesterol, blood pressure, and macular degeneration vitamins. I tried to help him by making healthy meals and to encourage him to go for walks since he did not like to exercise and so I just made good meals and stopped nagging him about the other. He kept blaming me and my cooking for his weight issues.

Apparently (in a feeling guilty moment) he did confess to me that he would get fast food while out on his jobs. He said he was trying to stop, but it was hard.

During that summer he started feeling tired a lot and when he mowed or did anything that was causing exertion, he would have burning across his chest area. He would have to stop and sit every few minutes. Against his wishes, I hired someone to mow the lawn. He finally confessed he was glad and besides it was someone he knew and could talk about stuff with that he did not share with me.

I soon found out that he had some health issues that he hid from me and when he went for a stress test, they wanted him to go immediately to the hospital, so I came home from my own medical appointment and took him, not knowing this was the last time I would be with him! Now he is gone—meaning he had an artery procedure and died on the operating table. The doctor came out and told me how bad off he was and if he did not have the procedure, he did not have long to live anyway. I actually had to ask him if my husband had died because the doctor would not say. I felt his bedside manner sucked, and in shock, I called my kids then drove home against the nurses wishes, but I had enough of that hospital and did not want to go back there.

In our marriage, he was fondly thought of as a wonderful stepfather and grandfather, so when he passed the whole family was shocked. My children were a big help in getting through all the funeral stuff. A lot of friends and family on both sides came and it was comforting.

I spoke to an attorney about the fact that he was not sent to a cardiologist before any procedures were performed. His new primary physician thought his chest burning was indigestion and put him on antacids for a couple months and when that did not solve the problem put him on nitro tablets, which should have been done after seeing a cardiologist. So, I will not get closure until I get some answers.

While all of this was going through my mind, I had to get myself together and get all the financial papers in order and figure out what he left me with to solve that I had no clue about. It was quite the challenge, and I found a lot of things about him that I did not know.

Now I am trying to go on without him. He was number three in my life, and it is true that some say that is a lucky number, but not so lucky when the love of your life and your best best friend dies, and you still feel something was not solved so I can move on the next chapter of my "LIFE UNEXPECTED"